Praise for *Meaningful Graphs*

"Dr. Smith's book, *Meaningful Graphs*, is a terrific resource for clinical, quality, and other healthcare professionals who have responsibility for presenting data as a component of their professional activities. I had the great privilege of working with Dr. Smith during a period of fundamental transformation in the Veterans Health Administration. Data were part of the journey, and effective presentation of the data provided fuel for that journey. Dr. Smith was the 'go to' guy for advice on how to present data effectively to facilitate understanding and motivate change. Now his expertise is available for all of us in this terrific reference guide, written in a conversational tone, for novice as well as more experienced Excel user. *Meaningful Graphs* is like having a wise colleague at your side helping you create effective graphs."

— **JONATHAN B. PERLIN**, MD, PhD, MSHA, FACP, FACMI, former Under Secretary for Health, US Department of Veterans Affairs

"There are so many good things in this book that it would be impractical to list them all. Suffice it to say that if you want to create charts and have Excel phobia or if you've got the data but you are failing to get your point across, this book is written for you."

—**MIKE DAVIDGE**, Director, NHS Elect, part of the National Health Service, London, England

"*Meaningful Graphs* is an important and valuable book for all who are leading a Lean or continuous improvement transformation in hospitals, or any industry. The book shows you how to more clearly represent trends about your improvement work, preventing confusion or statistical malpractice. I highly recommend this book for its insight as well as its practical tips for using Excel, a tool we all have, to help you create meaningful graphs as part of your meaningful work."

—**MARK GRABAN**, author of *Lean Hospitals* and co-author of *Healthcare Kaizen*

"As a lifelong health care educator, this book is one of the best educational tools I have ever encountered. It is an outstanding aide to people (especially health care professionals) interested in using Excel graphs in reports and presentations. The text and graphs are very clearly presented, the Tips and How To sections are extremely useful, and the myriad health care examples effectively complete the task of tying theory to practice."

—**JULES M. RANZ**, MD, Clinical Professor
of Psychiatry, Director, Public Psychiatry
Fellowship, NYS Psychiatric Institute/
Columbia University Medical Center

"*Meaningful Graphs* offers what most books do not: it cuts clear to the chase on what you need to do to create Excel charts that tell your story. It also includes user-friendly discussions of quality improvement and statistics as they relate to charts, and touches on PowerPoint techniques including chart animation. A must read for anyone who wants to master Excel charts, starting at the most basic level."

—**LINDA DENKE**, PhD, RN, Day 1 Mental
Health-Founder; Manager of Nursing
Research, Medical City, Dallas TX

"Finally!! A book that I can recommend to students so they can appreciate the science and art of *Meaningful Graphs*. Dr. Smith skillfully combines the principles of good graph design and the techniques of Excel and does so in a way that is brilliantly illustrated and easy to follow. I will ensure our book-store has multiple copies on hand."

—**JAMES REGAN**, Ph.D., Director, Graduate
Psychology Program, Marist College

"This text is an excellent overview and snapshot using real life clinical exam-ples that guide students, faculty, and practitioners in how to highlight salient data points using graphics. It shows how to bring the meaningful essence of data to life."

—**JAMES L. HARRIS**, PhD, APRN-BC, MBA, CNL,
FAAN, Co-Editor of *Initiating and Sustaining the
Clinical Nurse Leader Role: A Practical Guide* (2nd ed)

"One of the biggest challenges in health care today is that we are data rich but information poor. Converting data into meaningful graphs that help inform decision making is an important skill. Dr. Smith, who has spent over 35 years in healthcare research and quality, has done a masterful job in this book of presenting the art of good graph design in a format that can be easily understood and immediately applied."

—**ROSE O. SHERMAN,** EdD, RN, FAAN,
Professor and Director, Nursing Leadership
Institute, Florida Atlantic University

"Whether trees falling in forests make a sound is debatable. But we all know that data presented in a way that is not readily grasped will have no impact. Dr. Smith has mastered the art of sharing healthcare data in ways that are simultaneously rigorous and accessible to a wide audience. In *Meaningful Graphs,* Dr. Smith shares what he has learned, and I highly recommend this book."

—**LEWIS OPLER, MD,** PhD, Professor of Clinical
Psychiatry, Columbia University Medical Center

"Dr. Smith has done quite a job in creating this well-researched little gem on communication via graphs and charts. It is as much about understanding the communication one needs to make, in terms of delivering an accurate story line plus achieving the best viewer perceptual grasp; as it is about graphical choices, presentation styling and practical hints on how to achieve those results best. While he draws his illustrations from his long experience in health-care statistics, the caveats and recommendations are very easy to extrapolate into most other fields where quality graphical communication is important."

—**MICHAEL A. M. KEEHNER,** Adjunct
Professor, Finance and Economics, Bernstein
Faculty Leader, Columbia Business School

"Anybody, in any organization, planning to include quantitative data in a report . . . should first read this book."

—**MIKE CARBERRY,** Executive in Residence, Kogod
School of Business, American University

"Dr. Smith guides the reader to create knowledge from data, and to convey this knowledge in a clear concise manner."

—**SUSAN MACE WEEKS,** DNP, RN, CNS, LMFT, FAAN, Associate Dean, Harris College of Nursing and Health Sciences, Director, Center for Evidence-Based Practice & Research: A Collaborating Center of the Joanna Briggs Institute

Meaningful
Graphs

Meaningful Graphs

Converting Data into Informative Excel® Charts

JAMES M. SMITH, PH.D.

To my wife, Susan
For her constant love and support

To my children, Eileen, Kerry, and Elizabeth
For being the people they are

Contents

Appendices

Acknowledgments

First and foremost, I'd like to thank my colleague and friend, Dr. Allan Shirks, who read early drafts, provided encouragement, and gave very valuable insights. His attention to detail was greatly appreciated and his grasp of the big picture at times brought me back into focus when I badly needed this. I could not have asked for a better editor.

I also thank Dr. Thomas Craig, a friend and valued mentor, and Dr. Robert Murphy and Suzanne R. Murphy, who read drafts and made very helpful suggestions which greatly improved the final product. Davis Balestracci read the chapter on line charts and offered valuable insights into being cautious about drawing conclusions when observed effects may be due to normal process variation. Dr. Matthew Healy read the sections on statistics and made a number of valuable observations which I incorporated. Finally, I am greatly indebted to Stephen Few, who very generously volunteered to read a draft and offered helpful comments and suggestions that could only have been made by someone with his extensive knowledge of graph design.

My thanks to Dr. Jonathan B. Perlin and the *American Journal of Managed Care* for permission to reproduce Fig. 1 of an article which appeared in the November 2004 issue; to Jones and Bartlett for permission to reproduce Table 12-1, and Figs. 12-2, 12-5, and 12-6 from my chapter in *Initiating and Sustaining the Clinical Nurse Leader Role* by Harris, Roussel, and Thomas; to Ilya Levin for permission to reproduce the Pixie icon; and to The National World War II Museum in New Orleans for permission to present one of the displays from this museum. I also owe my gratitude to several people and organizations for stories, published data, or pictures that I used to make certain points: Philip Moschitta, Director and JoAnne

Anderson RN MSN of the Northport VAMC, Dr. Gretchen Van Wye, Dr. David Newman-Toker, and the National Aeronautics and Space Administration.

Finally, I'd like to thank the great staff and organizations with whom I've had the privilege to work: the New York State Office of Mental Health and the Veterans Health Administration. I have learned much from you about using data to effect positive change.

Preface

Over the course of my 35-year career in health care, I have seen thousands of graphs presented by quality improvement teams, nurses and other clinical professionals, performance measurement and program evaluation staff, patient safety professionals, facility administrators, fiscal managers, researchers, and a host of others. Some of these graphs were created by those directly involved and some by computer professionals familiar with software graphing packages. *I have always been amazed by how many of these graphs could have been vastly improved if only the basics of graph design had been known.*

Mistakes in the selection and formatting of graphs are very common not only in health care but in other settings as well: in newspapers and trade magazines, online, in financial reports, in presentations and poster sessions, and sometimes even in scientific journals. These mistakes include using the wrong type of graph for the information to be conveyed, employing graph types that are known to mystify rather than inform, truncating an axis when it shouldn't be truncated, and using colors without a purpose, to name just a few. What's the reason for this state of affairs? Few (2004) places some of the blame on the advent of the personal computer, noting that "when chart-producing software hit the scene, especially electronic spreadsheets, many of us who would have never before attempted to draw a graph suddenly became Rembrandts of the X and Y axes, or so we thought" (p. 5).

Designing a really effective graph, one that quickly and easily conveys the critical information, is a deliberative process. The keys to this process lie in knowing the answers to four critical questions:

A. What *type of graph* is best for displaying the information I want to display?

B. What are the *general principles of graph design* that apply to nearly all graphs?

C. What are the *specific principles of graph design* that apply to the particular type of graph I have chosen?

D. What are the software steps required to change the *format of my graph* so that it accords with the principles of good graph design?

The answers to these questions are not hidden. They can be found in numerous comprehensive books on graph design and on software. However, I know that many don't have the time to read all-inclusive books on graph design and software to cull the nuggets of information that relate to their own circumscribed use of graphs.

Based on my experience, I'm convinced that there is a need for *a single concise source of practical information that incorporates both the principles of good graph design and the software steps necessary to incorporate these principles into the graphs you create*. This book is designed to meet that need, a field manual, if you will, containing the basics of both good graph design and software techniques, that can be easily read, applied, and referenced. If you learn and apply the principles and techniques contained in this book, you will create meaningful graphs that effectively communicate your message.

Since this book is written for an audience who overwhelmingly use Microsoft Excel to create their graphs, the discussion will be limited to that software program. What I have been referring to as "graphs," Excel classifies as "charts," a term generally used more broadly to refer to any form of graphical display, including graphs, tables, and diagrams. Because the intent of this book is to show how to incorporate principles of graph design into the creation of Excel charts, I will use the term "chart" hereafter to refer to graphs.

Books on Chart Design

There are many fine books written on principles of chart design. Each of these is good in its own way. Some are better organized than others, some are more comprehensive, some are more technical and academic, some focus on historical displays, some focus on ineffective or misleading charts, some include information on the visual and cognitive underpinnings of good design, and some focus on the broader topic of information visualization. They are very informative and even enjoyable. As the many citations in the text attest, this book could not have been written without the comprehensive and definitive work found in these books. However, most are too comprehensive for those for whom chart design is an occasional task among many other priorities.

One of the most fundamental decisions in writing a book on charts is the determination of what types of charts to include. Since the focus of this book is on creating charts in Excel, that decision was an easy one. All the chart types and variations available in Excel 2010 are included. All other types of charts (e.g., bullet, box-and-whisker, waterfalls, funnels, tree maps, Nightingale roses), some useful and some not, are excluded because they are too numerous and sometimes quite technical, and most are available only with software add-ins to Excel or through complex procedures in Excel.

The major focus is on the five most frequently used chart types: column, bar, line, pie, and scatter. I refer to these as the Big Five. Believe it or not, many of the obvious charting mistakes occur with these basic charts. There are a number of other chart types in Excel, six to be precise, to which I devote less attention. Most of these are not very useful. Despite this, they are included since it is important to know what they are and how they should be interpreted when you see them used.

Writers on chart design have different personal preferences when it comes to design issues, and sometimes these are expressed rather strongly in words such as "dumb," "mumbling," "hateful," "mortal sin," and even "deserving of a special place in the inferno." Aside from not wanting to be in that special place in the inferno, my own personal preferences gravitate toward a "minimalist" school of chart design where the "wow!" factor comes from the clarity and precision with which the critical information is displayed rather than from the dazzling array of software-enabled enhancements that can be applied (exploding pie segments, 3-D effects, plot fill gradients, and the like).

While I adopt a minimalist approach to the display of scientific, health care, and quality improvement data, this is not to say that some of the chart types and software-enabled embellishments that I dismiss may not have value in other settings such as sales and marketing, venture capital, and public relations, to name just a few. In these settings special effects to produce attention-getting charts may be important for their audience. For those who, because of customer need, practice in their field, or personal preference, choose to vary from the principles espoused in this book, perhaps what I write will serve as a benchmark, akin to a budget. You don't always have to stay within the limits, but it's helpful to know when you've gone over them.

Books on Excel

Knowing the type of chart to use and the best format options for that particular chart is one thing. Knowing how to use Excel software to incorporate these changes in your own charts is something else again.

As with books on chart design, there are many fine books on Excel and some specifically on the Excel charting function. Given the complexity of Excel, these books are usually lengthy and quite technical. While they offer comprehensive coverage of all the diverse software options, most provide comparatively little in the way of guidance from a design perspective.

Since some reading this book may have never personally created a chart in Excel, I start my discussion of formatting at the most

IN PRACTICE

Let's be honest. In all fields, charts are sometimes intentionally drawn to obfuscate or mislead. Recently I saw a column chart of a hospital's performance in relation to a standard. It showed the hospital in a very good light— a light which would have nearly disappeared had the chart been properly drawn.

fundamental level. Beginning in Chapter 4 on column and bar charts and continuing in Chapter 5 on formatting, I work through the creation of a column chart from start to finish, modifying it as necessary. In addition, in a number of chapters I have included how-to sections indicating how changes have been made to the charts presented. As you'll see, changing some of the basic formats of a chart is quite easy. Finally, I have included an appendix that provides an overview of the vast array of chart format options available in Excel. There are also other appendices to address specific Excel chart format issues.

The chart examples in this book were all created in PowerPoint since it generates Excel spreadsheets with sample data already populated and avoids discussions of how to set up and manipulate spreadsheets. Chart formatting options and techniques are the same whether the chart is created in PowerPoint or in Excel. The information on changing chart formats is based on the 2010 versions of PowerPoint/Excel.

If you become familiar with the sections related to Excel formatting techniques, you will know the basics of how to make changes in your own charts to incorporate the principles of good design. It should be noted, however, that Excel is a complex program, and many more formatting options are available than I am able to cover in this book. If you have no desire or need to create and modify your own charts, you can skip the sections on Excel formatting techniques; the principles of good chart design alone should help in your discussions with the staff who create your charts.

Chapter Overview

Chapter 1, "Before You Create a Chart," highlights the importance of being clear about the information you want to convey. If you're not clear about this, you shouldn't be surprised if your charts are confusing. Chapter 2 contains a brief overview of chart terminology, the types of charts available in Excel, and a flowchart of when to use each of the five major chart types (column, bar, line, pie, and scatter). This flowchart is not all inclusive but covers the major decision points. Chapter 3 presents general principles of good chart design that apply to nearly all charts. Among the topics covered in this chapter are mental gymnastics in charts, chartjunk, the use of color, and a consideration of the use of 3-D effects. Since charts are often included in PowerPoint presentations, I've also included two general guidelines related to their use in PowerPoint.

After these three initial chapters, chapters are devoted to each of the Big Five chart types. Since column and bar charts are closely related, they are both covered in Chapter 4. Chapter 5 demonstrates how easy it is to change the format of chart elements using a column chart developed in Chapter 4. Line, pie, and scatter charts are covered in Chapters 6, 7, and 8, respectively.

Chapters 9 and 10 are devoted to descriptions of less frequently used types of charts: area, stock, surface, doughnut, bubble, and radar. Most of these chart types are confusing rather than enlightening, but a couple have value in certain situations. Chapter 11 concludes with some final thoughts on charts and on improving your skills in this area.

Chapters on the most useful chart types begin with a practical application of the chart's use; there are also numerous other chart examples throughout the text. Many of these examples include a table of data so that you can replicate and modify the chart on your own computer. Practice is important.

Since my background is in health care settings, nearly all of the examples presented are from the health care area. Nonetheless, the points I make about chart selection and design apply equally well to other areas. Illustrative examples could just as easily have been taken from strategic business planning, manufacturing, sports, personnel management, and a host of other areas. Had I known more about these areas, I would have included some examples from them.

In connection with several chart types, I've included a discussion of quality improvement techniques or statistical concepts since the chart type naturally lends itself to these discussions. Such is the case with column/bar charts and Pareto charts, line charts and run charts, and scatter charts and correlations.

Some Caveats. While it is essential to have everything properly labeled in a chart (chart title, axis titles, and the like), this is not done in many of the examples in this book because the point of the example is to demonstrate a chart effect and not to communicate specific results. In addition, some of these examples use more intense colors or larger fonts to demonstrate the point than those you would typically use in a report or presentation.

• • • • • • •

Despite my emphasis on the importance of charts and chart design, it goes without saying that no chart, no matter how well executed, will make up for a poor story line. Some feel that if they only knew more about the ins and outs of charts, they'd have a much more informative and engaging report or presentation. The most critical factor in creating a great report or presentation is the story line, keeping in mind that your story line must be verified by appropriate statistical techniques and not created by the artful manipulation of a chart to create a dramatic story where none exists. If you spend the time to develop your story line, you can use your skills with charts to get it across to your audience. Of course, the more you know about chart design, the better job you'll do. But make no mistake: The story line comes first.

Now for some practical advice: The rules are the rules but your boss is your boss. This book explains what the experts have to say about charts—the "rules for charts," so to speak. As you'll see, these experts discourage the use of several types of charts that are very popular. If your boss really, really likes one of these disparaged chart types and tells you to use it despite what the experts say (and what you know after reading this book), *just do it*. There's no sense losing your job over an exploded pie chart slice.

Before You Create A Chart

What does it take to create a really informative chart? Stephen Few, who is the author of some of the best books on chart design, puts it this way: "Excellent graph design is much like excellent cooking. With a clear vision of the end result and an intimate knowledge of the ingredients, you can create something that nourishes and inspires" (Few, 2012, p. 257).

Two elements are essential: knowing the information you want to communicate and knowing how to convey that information with charts. This chapter will share some thoughts on the first component, being clear about the information you want to communicate. The remainder of this book is devoted to the second component, chart selection and design.

A chart is effective only if it conveys the information that is most important to communicate based on the judgment of the content area expert and the needs of the intended audience. Giving your data to a chart expert and asking him to create a chart is like giving a chef multiple ingredients and asking him to make something. You'll get something, but it may not be what you want. If you're the subject matter expert and you are not designing the chart, collaboration with the chart creator is essential. You must meet with the person creating your chart and communicate what information is most important to you and to your audience.

An Illustration

Here's a concrete example of being clear about the information you want to convey. A clinic manager is interested in keeping track of the number of patients who are newly enrolled in the clinic ("enrollees") as well as those who have dropped out of the clinic ("attrition"). The clinic manager speaks to the organization's chart creator about creating a chart of enrollees and attrition for each of the past 12 months.

Clinic Manager: "I'd like you to create a chart of the monthly new enrollees and attrition to my clinic over the past year. I would consider someone to be an attrition if they haven't visited the clinic within the previous 12 months."

Chart Creator: "Sure, Boss. We have these data, and it should be relatively easy to create the chart you want. I'll be up later with it so you can take a look at it."

Sometime later . . .

Chart Creator: "Here it is, Boss. Just what you wanted: attrition and enrollees each month for the past year. There's not much pattern here, but if you want this on a regular basis, we can do it."

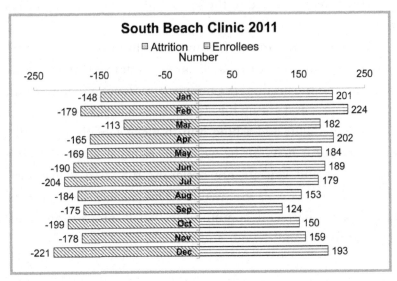

Fig. 1.1. Paired Bar Chart with Pattern Fill (Smith, 2013, reprinted with permission)

Pretend that you're the clinic manager. Take a minute and examine the chart in Fig. 1.1. Observe what you are doing as you look at it. What would you say about it to the chart creator? Would you ask the chart creator to make any changes?

Clinic Manager: "That's great. I can't believe how quickly you did this. But my eyes keep going back and forth, looking at the enrollees and attrition for each month."

Perhaps you had the same experience with your eyes automatically going back and forth. Many people do. *One of the first rules of charts is that if you have to do any mental gymnastics to get the information you want from a chart, it's not a good chart.*

Chart Creator: "I see what you mean, Boss. No problem. I can put the attrition and enrollees for each month next to each other."

Sometime later . . .

Chart Creator: "Here it is, Boss. The attrition and enrollees right next to each other for each month. Just what you wanted."

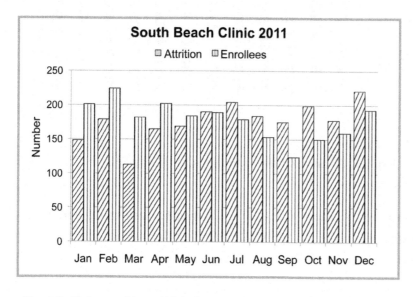

Fig. 1.2. Column Chart With Pattern Fill

Examine the revised chart in Fig. 1.2. What would you say about it to the chart creator? Would you ask for any changes?

Clinic Manager: "Well, that's better, but the patterns are confusing to my eye. Can you make them a little more distinctive?"

Chart Creator: "Sure, Boss. I'll be up with a revised version."

Sometime later . . .

Chart Creator: "Here it is, Boss. I used black columns for the attrition and gray columns for the enrollees to make them easier to distinguish. Just what you wanted."

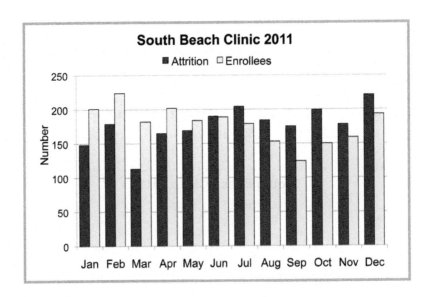

Fig. 1.3. Column Chart With Black and Gray Fills

Examine the chart in Fig. 1.3. Do you see any trend here that you didn't see in the two previous charts? What would you say about it to the chart creator?

Clinic Manager: "Thanks. That's a lot better. Now I see a trend in the data that I didn't see before. The Enrollees, the gray bars, seem to be going down while the Attrition, the black bars, seem to be going up."

Chart Creator: "You interested in trends, Boss? Why didn't you say so? Trends are lines, Boss. I can make a line chart of these data for you."

Sometime later . . .

Chart Creator: "Here it is, Boss, a line chart with lines for new enrollees and attrition. Just what you wanted."

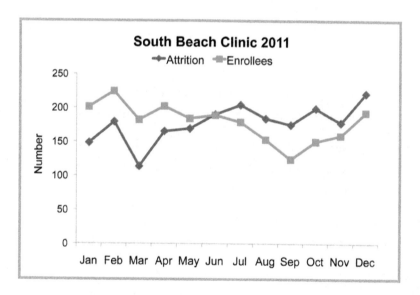

Fig. 1.4. Line Chart

Chart Creator: "I also made another line chart in which I truncated the y-axis at a value of 100 to emphasize the trends."

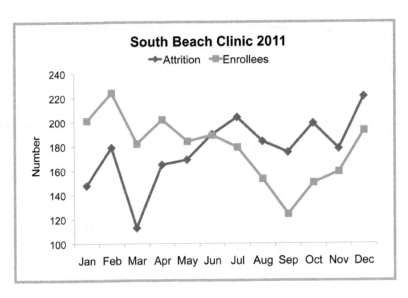

Fig. 1.5. Line Chart With Truncated Y-Axis

Examine the charts in Figs. 1.4 and 1.5. What would you say about them to the chart creator? Would you ask for any changes?

Clinic Manager: "The trends are more obvious now. I can see, for example, that we had many more enrollees than attrition in March but more attrition than enrollees in September."

Chart Creator: "Are you interested in seeing the difference between enrollees and attrition every month, Boss? I can do that."

Sometime later . . .

Chart Creator: "Here it is, Boss. A chart of the net change every month—enrollees minus attrition. Just what you wanted."

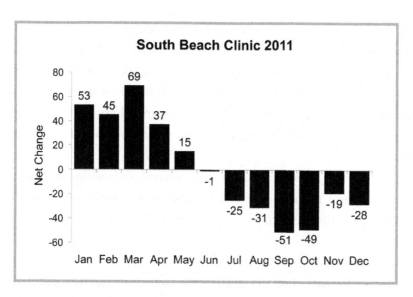

Fig. 1.6. Column Chart of Monthly Net Change (Smith, 2103, reprinted with permission)

Chart Creator: "And I did one for cumulative six-month periods as well."

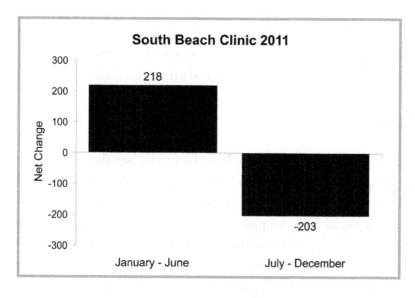

Fig. 1.7. Column Chart of Six-Month Net Change

At this point, the clinic manager excuses himself and goes to his office to update his resume. His clinic is clearly in trouble.

This sequence of charts, which used exactly the same data in each successive chart, illustrates the difference between **data** and **information**. Every single piece of data in the first chart of this sequence is in the last chart of this sequence and vice versa. But it's a changed picture.

The first chart presents data; this chart does nothing but induce confusion and malaise. The last chart presents information—information that induces change. *That's the difference between data and information.*

Had the clinic manager and the chart creator sat down at the outset to discuss what the desired information was, the discussion and chart iterations above would have been much abbreviated. Anyone who gives data to a chart creator and asks merely for a chart of the data will often be disappointed in the outcome.

Other Ways to Display Data

While this book is devoted to the use of charts, keep in mind that there are other ways to display data that, in some instances, are preferred over charts. The two main options for displaying data in a format other than charts are tables and other visualization techniques.

Tables

Few (2012) notes that tables should be used when the purpose of the data display is to look up values, to compare values precisely, to show values for variables involving different units of measure, and to present both detail and summary measures. For those seeking to learn more about tables and how they should be designed, Few (2012) has two chapters on the construction of tables, "Fundamental Variations of Tables" and "Table Design," which will improve your ability to communicate information clearly with tables.

Other Visualization Techniques

Visualizing information in formats other than charts and tables can run the gamut from simple to quite complex—all with the intent of making information more readily understandable. On one end, unidimensional visual displays can be used to communicate information on a single variable. On the other end, complex multidimensional infographics present many different types of data. They may incorporate charts, tables, pictures, illustrations, diagrams, maps, icons, symbols, and any other visual to provide information and insight into complex topics (events, systems, machinery, methods, and the like).

Often complex infographics can be found in newspapers and magazines. These are created by a staff of graphic journalists and other specialists who spend considerable time and effort to understand a complex phenomenon and then display it in a visual format that makes it more readily understandable by those who view it. Cairo (2013) notes that not only do complex infographics allow observers to perceive objects, events, and relationships quickly and easily but also sometimes allow users to answer questions that may be of interest only to themselves.

Cairo's book (2013) presents examples of outstanding infographics; books by Malamed (2009) and Tufte (1990) also provide examples. If you conduct a Google Image search on the topic "infographics" or specifically, "medical infographics," you'll see a wide array of these but be warned: a few are good but many are very poor. As Cairo (2013) notes,

> A simple Google search on *infographics* will return thousands of links to projects in which the designer didn't choose graphic forms according to how well they assist thinking, but because they looked cool, innovative, or funny. (p. 39, italics in original)

Here's a very simple but compelling example of the effect of visualizing data on a single variable. I discovered it several years ago on

IN PRACTICE

A complex infographic of storm damage from a hurricane along a coastline may involve a detailed map with separate symbols indicating the presence and extent of damage due to flooding, fire, wind and power loss. This would enable the viewer to see not only the overall pattern of damage but also to determine whether his/her area was affected more or less than others and in what specific regard.

a visit to a great museum, The National World War II Museum in downtown New Orleans (www.nationalww2museum.org). The very first exhibit you see in the section devoted to the European campaign is pictured in Fig. 1.8.

Fig. 1.8. Size of Standing Armies at the Start of World War II

This display shows the size of the standing armies of Japan, the United States, and Germany at the start of World War II. Each flag is made up of small, identically sized metal soldiers aligned in rows on shelves across the flag (note the horizontal rows in the picture). Figure 1.9 presents a close-up of the metal soldiers.

Fig. 1.9. Miniature Soldiers in the Flag Display

Each metal soldier represents 2,000 men in uniform at the start of World War II. The more men in uniform, the more metal soldiers required to create the flag and hence the larger the flag. The actual numbers of men in uniform at the start of WWII were Japan, 4.6 million; United States, 635,000; and Germany, 4.5 million. This display shows in a striking fashion how grossly undermanned the United States was at the start of the war.

The display from the World War II Museum is a very simple, albeit compelling infographic; it communicates a single fact, the differences among countries in their standing armies at the start of WWII. I could have seen a table of these numbers or even a column chart of these numbers and would have been impressed with the differences, but this impression would have faded, perhaps even by the time I had seen the remaining displays in the museum. But this flag image stayed with me. It has a visual and emotional power that tables and charts just don't have.

In some instances where emotional impact is important, you might want to give some thought to displaying your information in a way other than a chart or table. Malamed (2009) writes: "Precise charts and tables help to structure information so audiences can easily absorb the facts. When we wish to instigate a call to action, we find that emotionally charged imagery is the most memorable" (p. 12).

In their book *Switch*, Heath and Heath (2010) provide a good example of the power of a non-chart, non-tabular display of data. Jon Stegner, the procurement manager at John Deere, was convinced that the consolidation of purchasing contracts, currently negotiated independently by each of Deere's 14 factories, would save money. But he also realized that it would be difficult to convince each factory to give up their local control. To illustrate how wasteful this process was, Stegner asked a student intern to visit each of the factories and obtain samples of the different types of work gloves they purchased along with the price paid.

Stegner placed all the work gloves (a total of 424) on a table, tagged with the factory that made the purchase and the price paid. He then invited all division presidents to go through the pile of gloves, locating the ones purchased by their division, and comparing the price they paid with what others paid. The division presidents were scandalized by the number of gloves and the price variations, sometimes for the exact same gloves, and agreed to consolidate this process. The result was a reduction of suppliers from six to one and a reduction in the cost of work gloves by 50%. As Stegner put it, "This worked because we made it real to senior management, and by making it real and tangible, they were absolutely incensed" (Handfield, 2004).

SUMMARY

Charts can be very powerful in communicating information if (a) you are clear about the information you want to convey and (b) they are well designed. Tables should be used if there is a need to look up values, to compare values precisely, to show values for variables involving different units of measure, or to present both detail and summary measures. If you feel you have the need for a greater emotional appeal, consider other ways to display the information. If you want to learn more about the complex process of infographics, Cairo's book (2013) is an excellent resource.

2

Overview of Chart Types and Variations

Excel 2010 offers a dazzling array of chart choices. There are 11 distinct chart types and multiple variations available within each of these types—a total of 73 chart options. I like charts—charts are a good thing—but this is just too much of a good thing. The challenge is to pick, from among this vast array, the best chart type and specific variation to convey the desired information.

Naomi Robbins (2005) presents a simple rule for selecting the most effective chart: "One graph is more effective than another if its quantitative information can be decoded *more quickly or more easily by most observers*" (p. 6, italics added).

Kosslyn (2006) puts it similarly:

A graph is successful if the pattern, trend, or comparison it presents can be immediately apprehended. Our visual systems allow us to read proportional relations off simple graphs as easily as we see differences in the heights of people, colors of apples, or tilts of pictures mishung on the wall. (p. 4)

Instinctive recognition is what you are aiming to achieve in your chart selection and design. The good news is that when Naomi Robbins's rule is applied to data typically presented in a health care or other

IN PRACTICE

I spent a considerable portion of my career conveying performance results to line staff in healthcare facilities. It was critically important that these results be quickly and easily understood. If the measures themselves or the presentation of feedback were overly complex or obtuse, I would lose the line staff. Line staff are the engine for change. If you lose the line staff, you've lost your engine for change.

applied setting, only a relative handful of the 73 Excel chart options meet the criterion of being able to convey information quickly and easily to most observers.

Elements of a Chart

Figure 2.1 illustrates the basic elements of a chart. Knowing this terminology will help in later discussions.

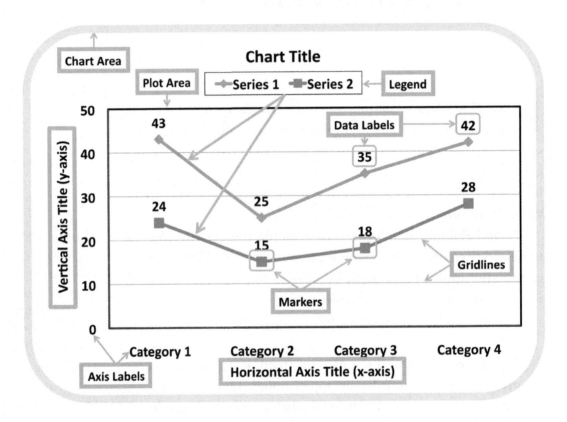

Fig. 2.1. Basic Elements of a Chart

A note about chart axes. The horizontal axis is *always* referred to as the x-axis, regardless of its content. It will frequently include category or time-based labels, but it may also consist of a scale for obtained values (bar and scatter charts). The vertical axis is *always* referred to as the y-axis. Often it will contain a scale for obtained values, but it may also consist of category labels (bar charts).

Chart Types

The first decision you need to make is to select the correct chart type to display the information you wish to communicate. This is critical. As Few (2013) notes, "A poorly chosen graph can completely obscure otherwise clear data" (p. 119).

There are four major types of information needs:

A. **Static Comparisons Among Discrete Categories**— "How does the rate of falls differ among hospital wards for a given quarter?"

B. **Trends Over Time**—"Has the rate of falls changed over the course of a year?"

C. **Proportions (Parts of a Whole)**—"Of all falls over the course of a year, what proportion were due to each of the various causes?"

D. **Relationships Between Variables**—"Is the rate of falls related to the average staffing level?"

It should be noted that some chart types can be used for more than one of these information needs. For example, column charts may be used for static comparisons among discrete categories and for trends over time for a limited number of time intervals.

HOW-TO. To see the array of chart types available in Excel, open a blank slide in PowerPoint | Insert | Chart. An Insert Chart box will appear with a menu of the names of 11 different chart types displayed vertically down the left side, starting with column charts.

Next to each of the 11 types are thumbnail pictures of the variations of that chart type available in Excel. If you hover the mouse pointer over each of these thumbnail pictures, its name will be displayed. Scroll down to see the variations available for all 11 chart types.

If you highlight a specific chart type and variation and click "OK," two windows will appear. The window on the left will contain a sample chart; the window on the right will display a spreadsheet with sample labels and data for the chart. To create a chart with your own data, simply replace the sample labels and data with your own labels and data, expanding or contracting the data field on the spreadsheet as necessary. To work on formatting the resulting chart, expand the window on the left so that it occupies the entire screen. If at some point you want to return to the data sheet, right click on the chart, choose Edit Data, and the spreadsheet will reappear.

The Big Five

Of the 11 chart types available in Excel, five—the Big Five—are the ones most frequently used (column, bar, line, pie, and scatter). Nearly everyone has seen or created one or more of these types of charts, and they will be covered in detail in later chapters. Brief descriptions along with their common uses are presented below.

Column charts are primarily used to convey data on discrete categories (hospitals, wards, clinics, etc.). They can also be used to display data over time periods or successive sequences (e.g., consecutively admitted patients) but only for a limited number of time or sequence periods.

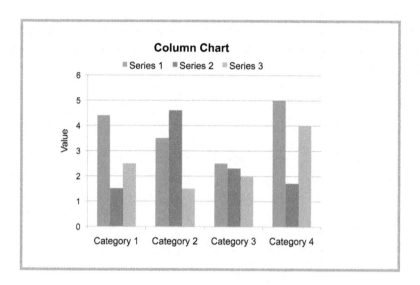

Fig. 2.2. Typical Column Chart

Bar charts can also be used to convey data on discrete categories. However, they are not suitable to convey trends over time.

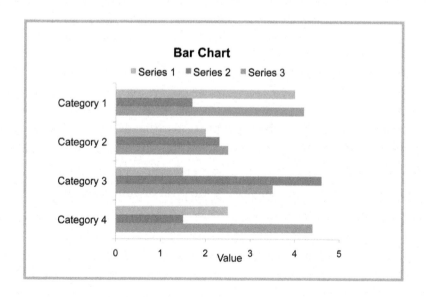

Fig. 2.3. Typical Bar Chart

While many authors refer to both vertical and horizontal orientations as bar charts, Excel refers to charts with a vertical orientation as column charts and charts with a horizontal orientation as bar charts.

Line charts are ideal for showing trends over time or successive events. They can be used for either short or long time periods/sequences.

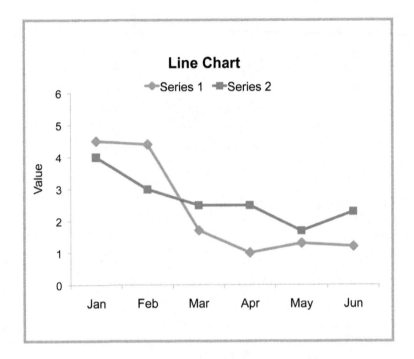

Fig. 2.4. Typical Line Chart

Pie charts are used to show proportions, that is, parts of a whole. Despite their widespread use and the natural appeal of a circle to convey a whole. As we'll see in Chapter 7 on pie charts, many experts on chart design feel that pie charts are poor at communicating information and suggest other alternatives.

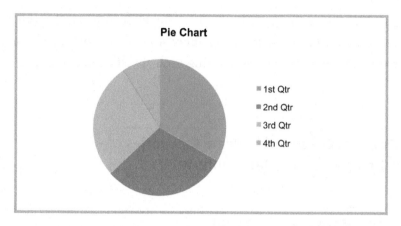

Fig. 2.5. Typical Pie Chart

Scatter charts are used to convey the relationship between two sets of values, one presented on the x-axis and one on the y-axis. The two variables may be on the same scale (e.g., triglyceride levels on split samples obtained on two laboratory machines) or on different scales (e.g., number of patient complaints and facility bed capacity for a number of hospitals).

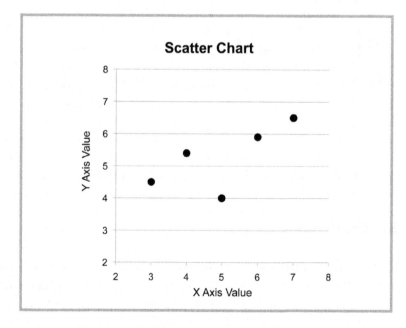

Fig. 2.6. Typical Scatter Chart

Figure 2.7 presents some basic rules for choosing among the Big Five. The rationales for the rules incorporated in this flowchart are explained in the chapters addressing each specific chart type.

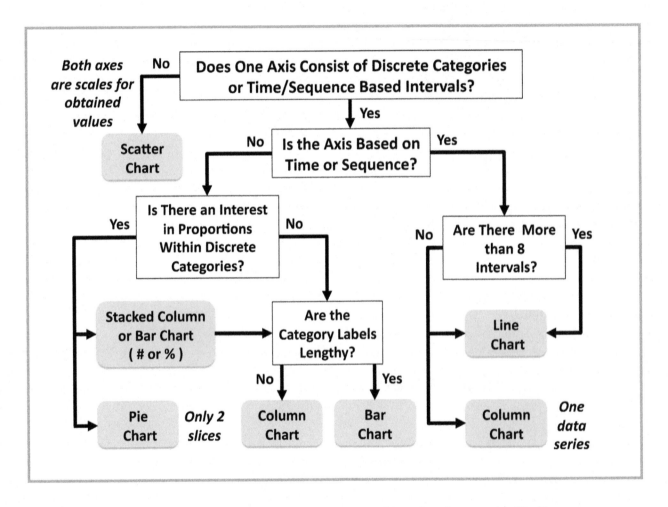

Fig. 2.7. Flowchart for Choosing Among the Big Five

Other Chart Types

The six less frequently used Excel chart types are displayed in Table 2.1. Some of these charts may be new to you. I hope I don't spoil the surprise when I tell you that in our discussion we will dismiss many—but not all—of these less frequently used charts.

Table 2.1. The Six Less Frequently Used Chart Types

TYPE OF CHART	ILLUSTRATION	COMMON USES
Area Chart		To show patterns and trends over time for either a small or large number of time periods
Stock Chart		To show stock price changes and other associated values (e.g., volume)
Surface Chart		To show values on three variables
Doughnut Chart		To show the proportion of components contributing to a total
Bubble Chart		To show the relationship among three variables
Radar Chart		To show values on a circular grid.

Chart Variations

In the Excel charts menu, the variations listed horizontally alongside each of the 11 types are created by modifying the basic type in some way. For example, in the case of column charts, variations are created by adding 3-D effects or replacing the typical rectangular columns with other shapes (cylinders, cones, or pyramids). The number of variations available for each of the 11 chart types range from a high of 19 for column charts to a low of 2 for doughnut and bubble charts. A complete listing of available chart variations by chart type may be found in Appendix A. Don't be dismayed by the multiplicity of these choices. As we will see, many of these variations do not contribute to, and sometimes impede, conveying information quickly and easily to most observers.

Once you have selected a chart type and a specific variation of that type, your work is not done. You then have to consider what particular formatting options to use for the various elements within the chart. Interestingly, some of the Excel chart default options are not good choices and need to be modified after the chart is initially created.

SUMMARY

As you can see, there are a multiplicity of options involving chart type, chart variation, and individual chart elements. If this process of chart creation seems overwhelming, don't panic. First, many of the chart types and variations will be eliminated in our subsequent discussions. Second, once you have a chart with options that you like, you can save this chart as a template to use again without having to recreate it element by element. As Few (2012) points out, when you get the hang of it, "it is no more difficult and takes no longer to produce effective tables and graphs than it does to produce ineffective ones" (p. 9).

3

General Guidelines

On the topic of communicating numeric information, Tufte (1983) writes,

> Often the most effective way to describe, explore, and summarize a set of numbers—even a very large set—is to look at pictures of those numbers. Furthermore, of all the methods for analyzing and communicating statistical information, well-designed data graphics are usually the simplest and at the same time most powerful. (p. 9)

The first and most important guideline is to select the type of chart and format that highlights the most important information, so that this information can be perceived quickly and easily by most observers. As we've seen, each specific type of chart is good at conveying a certain type of information—information about comparisons, or patterns/trends, or proportions of a whole, or interrelatedness—and, if you construct your chart well, the result will be as Tufte (1983) describes it: simple and powerful.

In this process, it may be necessary to experiment with several different ways of analyzing the data and several types of charts and formats until you find the right one. As Gladwell (2000) notes in a broader context, "There is a simple way to package information that, under the right circumstances, can make it irresistible. All you have to do is find it" (p. 132). Your aim should be to make your message *irresistible*, a format that allows you, as Few (2009) puts it, "to lift the veil that separates us from insight" (p. 2).

We'll spend considerable time going into detail about the distinctions among chart types and the specific formatting options for each, but in this chapter we'll present guidelines that apply generically, that is, across most types of charts.

Aspect Ratio

The aspect ratio is defined as the height of a chart compared to its width. The best aspect ratio depends on several factors, including the type of chart selected, the number of values in the chart, and what you most want to see in the data.

Chart Labeling

Charts should be clearly labeled. I know that this sounds like a "duh!" but if you look closely at charts published and presented, you'll be surprised by the many problems in this area. The chart title, axis titles, and axis labels should be self-explanatory. Your rule of thumb should be that if the page with only the chart on it fell from your report, anyone picking it up could easily tell what was depicted. Don't forget that the value axis (e.g., the y-axis in a column chart) should specify units of measurement.

In addition to the required text in a chart (chart title, axis titles, axis labels, and a legend if more than one series of data is presented), other text may be added to help convey important information. An example would be to use text to highlight an outlier or indicate in a time sequence where an intervention or special circumstance occurred that affected the charted phenomenon. Another example would be to clarify the meaning of a scale. Figure 3.1 shows examples of the use of additional text.

IN PRACTICE

Time series data are usually displayed in a rectangular (1 to 1.5) aspect ratio, while scatter charts are usually displayed in a square (1 to 1) aspect ratio.

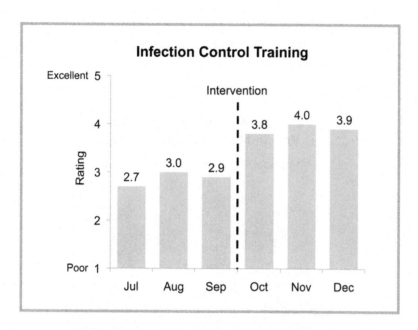

Fig. 3.1. Additional Text Added to a Column Chart

A dotted line and a text box with the word "Intervention" were added to show when the intervention took place. Also, the text boxes containing the words "Excellent" and "Poor" were placed alongside the y-axis to clarify the anchor points for this axis. We'll show how to add these elements in Chapter 4 (column and bar charts).

Mental Gymnastics

Sometimes a chart is constructed in a way that requires observers to do some mental rearrangements or calculations ("gymnastics," if you will) to get the information they want—visually transposing columns, mentally computing percentages, drawing imaginary lines along the tops of columns, and the like. *Simply put, if you have to do any mental gymnastics to get the information you want from a chart, it's not a good chart.*

Here's an example. Suppose the critical information you wanted to display was whether different medical specialties in your facility were discharging a greater percentage of patients within Medicare length-of-stay guidelines in 2010 as compared to 2008. The data could be presented in a chart as shown in Fig. 3.2.

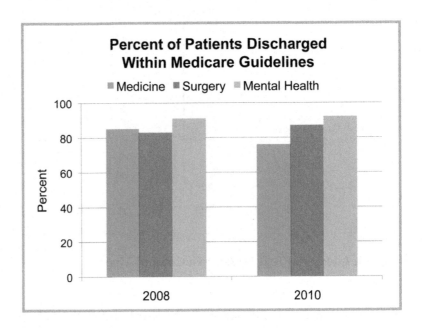

Fig. 3.2. Column Chart with Data Grouped by Year

Look at Fig. 3.2 and determine whether surgery discharged a greater percentage of patients within Medicare guidelines in 2010 than it did in 2008. In order to answer that question, you have to compare the height of red column on the right (2010) with the height of the red column on the left (2008). If you wanted to know whether the other services were doing better, you'd have to repeat this process for each of the other services—visually shifting back and forth between the respective service columns.

If the information of interest is to compare each of the services for the two periods, why not present the columns for the two years next to each other for each of the three services as in Fig. 3.3?

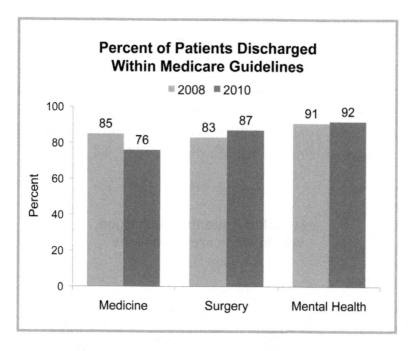

Fig. 3.3. Column Chart With Data Grouped by Service

As noted by Balestracci (2009), comparing averages such as these assumes that the temporal pattern over the 12 months of each of these two years is a random one, that is, one that shows no significant pattern or trend over time. If this is not the case, computing and comparing averages may be inappropriate and meaningless.

The answers about the progress of each of the services are now readily apparent since the columns of interest are adjacent to each other. Note also that the information value of this chart is enhanced by the use of data labels (the actual values) placed above their respective columns. We'll discuss how to add data labels in Chapter 5 (formatting chart elements).

Another example of mental gymnastics was apparent in Chapter 1 (Fig. 1.1), where monthly data on attrition and enrollees were compared using paired horizontal bars. As you may recall, the manager wanted to see whether the clinic was gaining or losing patients each month. To get this information from the data presented in Fig. 1.1, the manager had to look back and forth across the horizontal bars for each month. While some people may be familiar with this type of side-by-side bar chart and can obtain information from it, most observers who are not accustomed to this chart format find it difficult.

Data Labels and Data Tables

Data labels are the actual data values placed near the data points (e.g., on top of columns in a column chart or adjacent to data points in a line chart, as in Fig. 3.3). A *data table* is a listing of these data values in a matrix format beneath the chart (Fig. 3.4).

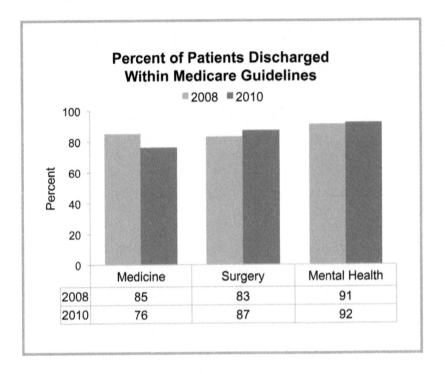

Fig. 3.4. Column Chart with a Data Table

The use of a data table beneath the chart requires the observer to pull together data from different areas in the chart: the heights of the respective bars from the chart itself and the actual values from the table beneath the chart. This requires mental gymnastics. In most instances, data labels should be preferred over a data table.

Chartjunk

"Chartjunk" is a term coined by Tufte in his 1983 book *The Visual Display of Quantitative Information*. It refers to all elements of a chart that do not convey information. This includes pictures and icons, background graphics, template material, shading and color for no purpose, redundant data, and the like. In this book Tufte introduced the concept of data-ink, based on the principle that "a large share of ink on a data graphic should present data-information, the ink changing as the data change" (Tufte, 1983, p. 93). Comparing the data-ink to the total ink used to produce the graphic, yields a conceptual data-ink ratio.

$$\frac{\text{data-ink}}{\text{total ink used to print the graphic}}$$

The higher the ratio, the greater the proportion of total ink devoted to data and the less unnecessary material the graphic contains. According to Tufte (1983), the goals should be to "maximize the data-ink ratio, within reason" (p. 96) and to "erase non-data-ink, within reason" (p. 96). "Within reason" is a key phrase since at times the addition of non-data-ink may allow observers to read charts more quickly. For our purposes, suffice it to say that you should consider removing all *unnecessary* material from a chart.

If you want to see some classic examples of chartjunk, take a look at the USA Today Snapshot charts on page 1 of this daily newspaper. They are usually about an interesting topic, are simple and colorful, and are typically loaded with chartjunk (background pictures, totally unrelated content, etc.). Though I enjoy looking at these charts, I wouldn't want to incorporate any chartjunk similar to this in a professional presentation.

Chartjunk is not merely confined to over-the-top elements gratuitously added to a chart; some is much more subtle. What's the chartjunk in Fig. 3.5?

TIP

If you're unfamiliar with the *USA Today* Snapshot charts, Google "USA Today Snapshot Archive," and you'll find numerous examples.

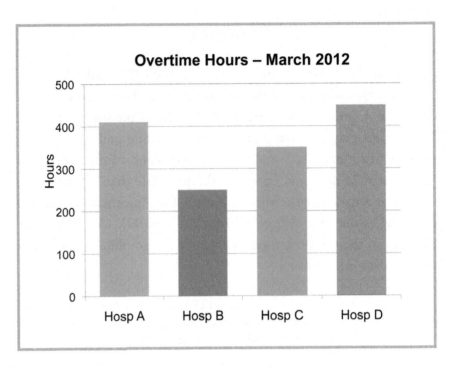

Fig. 3.5. Chartjunk—Illustration A

The different colors for each of the columns are chartjunk. Colored columns or different shades of the same color are used typically to denote different series of data (as in the Medicare discharge chart, Fig. 3.3), but in Fig. 3.5, in which there is only one series of data, the colors of the different columns have no meaning whatsoever. Even though they have no intentional meaning, sometimes colors have different psychological meanings (e.g., green = good, red = bad). I have no idea how the habit of coloring columns or bars different colors in a single series column or bar chart originated, but I see it used quite often.

What's the chartjunk in Fig. 3.6?

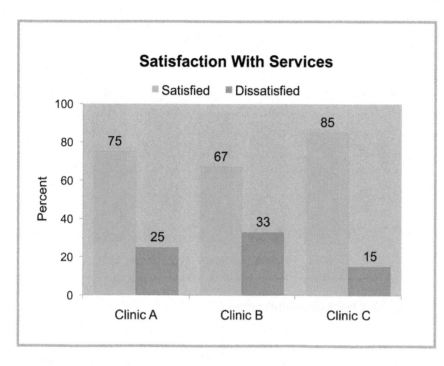

Fig. 3.6. Chartjunk—Illustration B

The plot area fill color (the background gray) is chartjunk. It has no meaning and sometimes makes a chart more difficult to read. But there's another, even more problematic, example of chartjunk in this chart.

Either the satisfied scores or the dissatisfied scores are chartjunk. Since the two scores for each clinic sum to 100%, if you know one, you automatically know the other. Presenting both values as part of the chart is unnecessary and distracting, forcing the reader to look at both series of data when one would suffice to convey the information. Whether you choose to present percent satisfied or percent dissatisfied is up to you.

What's the chartjunk in Fig. 3.7?

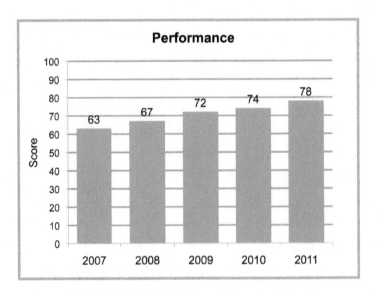

Fig. 3.7. Chartjunk—Illustration C

The gridlines are chartjunk. Gridlines are necessary to assist in estimating the values of each of the columns, but if data labels are used to show the actual values, there is no need for gridlines. Isn't this just nitpicking? Look at the chart in Fig. 3.8, where the gridlines have been removed, and answer that question for yourself.

TIP

Some consider "tick marks," the very short lines extending from the axis line to delineate the separation between successive categories or values, as a form of chartjunk since they don't convey any information. If that's the only form of chartjunk you have in your chart, you're doing fine.

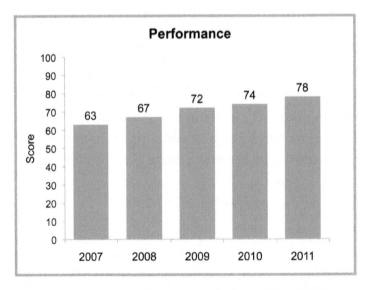

Fig. 3.8. Column Chart With Data Labels and No Gridlines

Three-Dimensional (3-D) Charts

Several chart types have variations that include a third dimension. In the simplest form of 3-D chart, columns and bars become blocks, pie charts have depth by being tilted slightly away from the viewer to display a thickness to the pie, and lines and areas become planes. In more complex 3-D displays, different series of data are presented from front to back along a third axis, referred to as the z-axis. These variations may be considered jazzy by some (evidently by many, judging by their frequency of use), but most experts agree that the third dimension is fraught with problems.

All charts can present problems in conveying information if used improperly. What makes the problem of 3-D charts unique is that their major failings are inherent in the chart design itself—namely, the confusion induced by the depth-of-field effect. Conveying a third dimension on a two-dimensional (2-D) surface creates difficulties for the eye and brain. Just look at some of the fantastic optical illusions that prey upon the brain's bewilderment when confronted with a 3-D simulated image on a 2-D plane.

One of the problems with 3-D charts is that the eye and brain automatically estimate the values of the columns from the grid in the background. Unfortunately, this gives a false reading since the actual height of the columns differs, sometimes appreciably, from the value read on the background grid. The reason for this visual distortion is that the 3-D column blocks are not right against the grid in the background but removed somewhat from it, even in a simple 3-D chart.

In a 3-D chart with multiple series of data presented from foreground to background, the confusion is even more dramatic. Look at Fig. 3.9. The tallest blue column (Ward 17W, Night) visually aligns near the gridline for 50 in the background. Believe it or not, the actual value of the tallest blue column is 65!

> **TIP**
>
> For a striking example of the confusion induced by displaying three dimensions on a 2-D surface, go to *http://www.moillusions.com/2009/06/audi-r8-optical-illusion.html*. In this picture of three cars, which car is larger?

TIP

If you find it difficult to believe that the blue column for Ward 17W, Night, has a value of 65, try this. Take a blank sheet of paper and place it vertically alongside the blue column. Mark the top and bottom of the front face in the center of this column on the blank sheet. Now move this sheet over to the grid on the side of the chart at approximately the same distance from the front as the column itself. Read the value from this side grid.

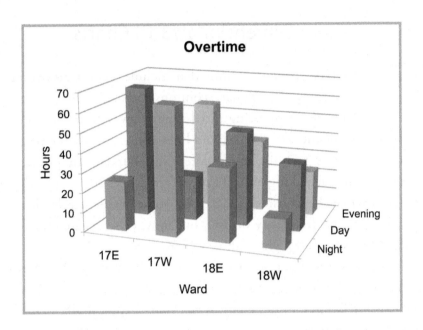

Fig. 3.9. Multiple Series 3-D Chart

A second problem with 3-D charts is data dependent. A higher value column in the foreground may totally obscure a lower value column in the background. Note in Fig. 3.9 how the blue column for Ward 17W, Night, totally obscures the green column for Ward 17E, Evening, (which has an actual value of 50).

A final problem with 3-D charts is that patterns and trends are much more difficult to identify in a 3-D chart with more than one data series. You have to work at it—something that well-designed charts don't require. Note in Fig. 3.10 how the immediately discernible and unique pattern of overtime for Ward 17W in the line chart is more difficult to discern in either 3-D version.

Although the use of 3-D charts is very common, most experts on chart design are very clear that they should be avoided, arguing that they are virtually unreadable (Robbins, 2005), sacrifice communication through the use of meaningless 3-D fluff (Few, 2012), obscure the data and direct the reader's attention away from the content (Wong, 2010), and are sometimes as confusing as Escher drawings (Kosslyn, 2006).

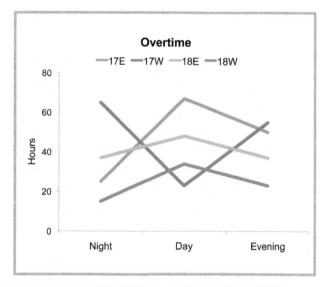

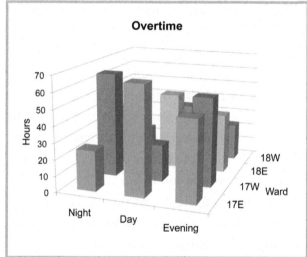
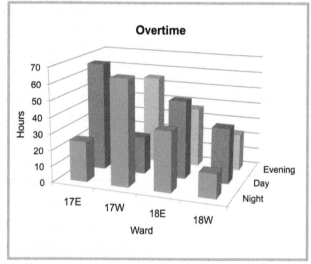

Fig. 3.10. Line Chart and Two 3-D Versions of the Same Data

Jones (2007) writes that "it's virtually impossible to make a 3D chart that doesn't give a wrong impression" (p. xvii). Jones continues: "Unfortunately, 3D bars are now the staple of the wildly popular 'dashboard' displays of executive information systems. Managers are actually making operational and strategic decisions based on this type of reporting. It's scary" (p. xviii).

Use of Color

Color serves three principal roles in charts. First, it can be used to differentiate among different series of data. We have already seen several examples of this use of color in column and line charts. Color is also very effective in distinguishing among different series of data plotted on a scatter chart (Cleveland, 1985; Few, 2012; Robbins, 2005).

A second use of color is to highlight an element or elements in a chart. Malamed (2009) notes that studies show that "when an area of a graphic is highlighted as it is being discussed, such as in a multimedia environment, viewers retain more information and are better able to transfer this information than those who did not view the highlighted visuals" (p. 73).

Saber Tehrani et al. (2013) analyzed data from the National Practitioner Data Bank (NPDB) to examine diagnosis-related claims (missed, wrong, or delayed) in comparison with other malpractice allegation claim groups. A subset of data found in Table 3 of this study was used to create Fig. 3.11 (this figure was not part of the original article). A darker shade of color was employed to highlight the percent of severe outcomes that were diagnosis-related, a category that accounted for nearly the same percentage of claims as the next two malpractice allegation groups combined.

Finally, colors either as fill or outline can be used as additions to a chart (text boxes, shapes, etc.) to ensure that attention is directed to the information highlighted. In using colors several principles should be kept in mind.

The use of bright colors in large areas of a chart produces sensory overkill and is distracting (Few, 2013). Lighter and less vivid shades should be used for chart elements with large areas (e.g., columns and bars). Tufte (1990) suggests using colors found in nature (blues, yellows, and grays) to represent and illuminate information, indicating that "a palette of nature's colors helps suppress production of garish and content-empty colorjunk" (p. 90). Few (2013) also recommends colors common in nature (soft grays, browns, oranges, greens, and blues) for information dashboards. On the other hand, smaller areas

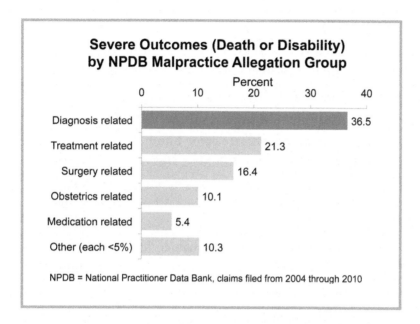

Fig. 3.11. Use of Color to Highlight Specific Chart Element (Data source: Saber Tehrani et al., 2013)

(e.g., lines and points in scatter charts) require more intense colors to be distinguishable. Bright colors or different shades of the same color can also be used to highlight specific elements in a chart (as in Fig. 3.11).

Other things to note about the use of color include the following:

- Different colors (hues) should not be used to convey quantitative differences. Different intensities of the same color can be used to convey quantitative differences, but our ability to detect intensity differences is limited (Few, 2012).

- Colors have inherent meanings for different groups of people, for the same groups of people in different circumstances, and for people from different cultures (Jones, 2007; Kosslyn, 2006). Financial managers view green as profitable, health care professionals view green

Although color may be very effectively used in charts for reports and presentations, most peer-reviewed journals do not allow the use of color in charts. If you're preparing something for publication, check the guidelines for authors for the journal to which you intend to submit. These guidelines are often found on the journal website.

IN PRACTICE

In a large hospital network in which I worked, the summary report of performance on a large number of measures was coded in red and green. Everyone referred to it as the "Christmas tree report." There was nothing wrong with this characterization, but it demonstrates the strong association of specific colors with particular holidays.

TIP

A useful website – *www.colorbrewer2.com* – presents color schemes for conveying quantitative and qualitative information. You can preselect for schemes that are colorblind safe, suitable for desktop color printing, or useful for black and white photocopying. Although designed for coloring map regions, the color selections may be helpful in other applications.

as infected or bilious, and control engineers view green as safe (Jones, 2007). In Western cultures, red is often used to denote problematic performance, but in China, red represents good fortune (Few, 2012).

- Some colors are problematic for the 10% of men and the 1% of women who are color-blind. The most common form of color blindness affects the ability to distinguish between red and green, one of the most frequently used palettes in dashboard reports. For those with red/green color blindness, the two colors appear brown and almost indistinguishable. People with red/green color blindness can, however, distinguish among different intensities of the same color (Few, 2013).

- If the presentation or report will be printed in black and white, it's a good idea to print a draft to see how the colors are rendered. If you can't use color and want to differentiate columns or bars, use shades of gray through black rather than different patterns. The visual shimmer sometimes induced by patterns has already been noted. With line charts, different line patterns (dashes, solid) can be used, along with different marker shapes, instead of color coding, though the latter is preferable.

Take the Nature of the Data Into Account

Sometimes the pattern of the data will help determine the best format for conveying the critical information. Wong (2010) indicates that you should limit line charts to four or fewer lines. That is probably often true, but the determining factor is the pattern of the data. A line chart for trends over 12 months for five different hospitals may be fine if the lines intersect very little. On the other hand, if the lines are close to each other and intersect frequently, a better option would be to have two separate charts (e.g., one with three hospitals and one with the other two) or as a cluster of small individual charts, one for each hospital.

Small Multiples. In some instances a pattern of effects may become clearer if it is portrayed with multiple individual charts (vertically, horizontally, or in a matrix format) rather than as one chart with several different series. Tufte (1983) coined the term "small multiples" to characterize this type of display, writing that "for a wide range of problems in data presentation, small multiples are the best design solution" (Tufte, 1990, p. 67). These arrays are also known as trellis, matrix, or multipanel displays. Small multiples can sometimes be quite effective in communicating information on values across three categorical variables.

If the aim of the small multiples display is to allow comparisons among all charts on the same variable, it is essential that the range of the value axis scales remain constant for all charts in the array. It is also important to arrange the multiple displays so they can be viewed simultaneously on a single page or computer screen. Since the overall pattern is most important, the size of each individual chart can be considerably reduced. Small multiples can be created using any of the chart types. Depending on the arrangement of the array, some axis titles and labels need not be repeated for some of the charts (Few, 2012; Kosslyn, 2006). Small multiples may also consist of different data sets (e.g., training time, staff accidents, and staff injuries for several different programs) as long as the arrangement of the small multiples drives the viewer to make appropriate comparisons. In his book *Show Me The Numbers*, Few (2012) has an entire chapter on displaying many variables at once.

Since charts are often used in PowerPoint presentations, we'll conclude with two general guidelines related to the use of charts in PowerPoint slides.

> **TIP**
>
> Don't assume that two or more charts on the same variable created for comparison purposes will have the same range for the value axis. Excel has a feature that automatically determines the range of the value axis based on the data. Sometimes this will invalidate visual comparisons among charts. In Chapter 5 we will see why this happens and how to prevent it from happening.

Slide Space

Let me begin by discussing PowerPoint (PPT) templates. I'm sure you know what PPT templates are. They're preformatted slide designs, backgrounds, color and font selections, and the like, that are used for all the slides in a presentation or in multiple presentations. Often the title slide has a unique pattern, design, or photo, and the remaining slides have a complementary design or pattern. Although PPT templates can be designed well to provide consistency within or across presentations (Swinford & Terberg, 2013), they are often poorly constructed. Swinford and Terberg (2013) note that "a *lot* of presentation templates cross our desks, and they all have problems!" (p. 1, italics in original). Despite this, PPT templates are big sellers. A recent Google search on the term yielded 8.4 million hits.

While PPT templates can be used effectively in a presentation or multiple presentations by providing uniformity of fonts, color selections, layouts, branding, and the like, many PPT templates involve a uniform picture or background graphic on every slide with areas restricted for borders, titles, and text. The latter templates are a distraction and often a waste of slide space.

Take a look at Fig. 3.12, a mockup illustration of a slide used to present new admission procedures on an intensive care unit (ICU).

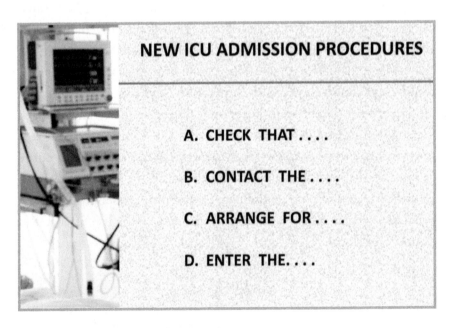

Fig. 3.12. Slide With Template

As soon as this slide is presented on the screen, you can bet that a number of people in the audience will *immediately* focus on the picture of the ICU equipment. Someone may even be thinking "That looks like the equipment we had in Building 14 before the building was renovated. Boy, that renovation was some mess. I remember when we tried to move the . . . ." By the time they refocus on what the speaker is saying, they've already missed the first point.

If you believe the advertisements claiming that their PPT templates can change your dull and boring presentation into a lively and vibrant presentation with little or no effort on your part, I have a bridge from Manhattan to Brooklyn to sell you. Once you put up toll booths, you can have a steady stream of income for the rest of your life!

Aside from serving as a distraction, templates take up space on the slides. Slide space is precious—don't waste it. Take a look at Fig. 3.13. It's similar to a slide I saw at a conference I attended several years ago. Notice how the plot area occupies just a small, central portion of this slide (specifically, only 15% of the total available slide space).

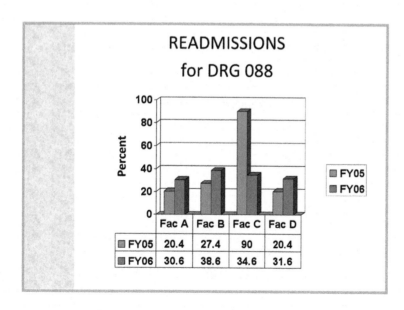

Fig. 3.13. Slide With Poor Use of Space

Imagine it's the end of a long and draining conference day, and you're sitting in the back of a large room. When this slide appears on the screen, you can barely make out the details. Instead of straining to see the chart, you give up and use your smartphone to search the Internet for a restaurant for dinner.

Fig. 3.13 is a classic example of poor use of slide space. What's wrong with it?

1. The blue border on the left hand side (akin to a template) may be a nice pattern for a countertop, but it's a total waste of slide space.

2. The overly large font for the title, requiring two lines, wastes space at the top of the slide.

3. The placement of the legend on the right side of the chart (the default legend placement in Excel) wastes space on the right hand side of the slide.

4. Finally, the data table beneath the chart wastes space at the bottom of the slide.

Now take a look at Fig. 3.14, a redrawn slide with the same data.

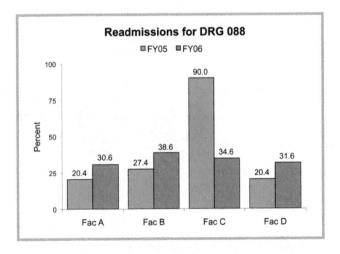

Fig. 3.14. Slide With Better Use of Space

In Fig. 3.14, the countertop border has been removed and the font for the title has been reduced in size so that it occupies only one line. The legend has been moved from the side of the chart to the top. Finally, the values of the columns have been placed above each column, as data labels, instead of being presented in a data table beneath the chart. Making these changes yields much more space for the chart plot area, which now occupies 49% of available slide space, more than three times the area occupied in Fig. 3.13. Which chart would you rather look at from the back of a large conference room?

HOW-TO. A PowerPoint slide provides 75.0 sq. inches of slide space to use. You know this because if you draw a rectangle (Insert | Shapes | Rectangle) to fit exactly over a blank PPT slide, click on this rectangle, and select Format, the ribbon will indicate that this rectangle is 7.5" tall by 10.0" wide. Knowing this, you can calculate how much slide space is used by any object on your slide. In Fig. 3.13, a box drawn to cover the chart plot area is 3.0" x 3.8" (11.4 sq. inches), 15% of the total available slide space (11.4/75.0). In contrast, in Fig. 3.14, a box drawn to cover the chart plot area is 4.6" x 8.0" (36.8 sq. inches), 49% of the total available slide space (36.8/75.0).

How to adjust font sizes, change the location of the legend, and add data labels will be addressed in Chapter 5.

Chart Animation

Every two years, Dave Paradi takes a survey of PowerPoint audiences to find what annoys them most about PPT presentations. In Paradi's latest survey (2013), 682 respondents picked their top three PPT annoyances. Overly complex diagrams ranked fourth most annoying: 31% of respondents selected this among their top three.

Sometimes a complex phenomenon requires a complex chart. However, when a complex chart is displayed, audiences may be

The top three PowerPoint annoyances in Paradi's survey are "the speaker read the slides to us" (72%), "text so small I couldn't read it" (51%), and "full sentences instead of bullet points" (48%).

overwhelmed by its complexity. They instinctively search for meaning in the chart while, at the same time, the presenter is doing his or her best to explain the chart. This dual approach to understanding often hampers comprehension. Frequently, a complex chart can be made much more understandable by introducing chart elements one at a time using animation. Appendix B explains how to animate charts the PowerPoint Chart Animation way and a clunky way.

SUMMARY

- Create charts with the aspect ratio that is most suitable to the data being presented.
- Label charts clearly.
- Avoid the need for mental gymnastics to interpret the chart.
- Favor data labels over a data table.
- Avoid chartjunk (nonessential elements).
- Avoid 3-D charts.
- Use colors judiciously.
- Take the nature of the data into account.
- In PowerPoint presentations,
  - ➤ Use slide space wisely.
  - ➤ Consider animating complex charts.

Displaying Discrete Categories: Column and Bar Charts

CHAPTER TOPICS

- When to use column and bar charts

- Why some Excel default settings are not optimal

- The use of column charts to display a trend over time

- How to use stacked and 100% stacked column and bar charts to facilitate the interpretation of data

- The construction and value of histograms and Pareto charts

- Dot plots: what they are and when they are useful

The primary purposes of column and bar charts are to present information on discrete categories (hospital, clinic, days of the week, age groups, etc.) or on trends over relatively short time intervals. Excel categorizes charts with vertical bars as "column charts" and charts with horizontal bars as "bar charts."

Column Charts

Clustered Column Chart

A clustered column chart presents data on discrete x-axis categories. If there are two or more series of data for each x-axis category, the data for each series are "clustered" above each category.

An Application

We'll begin our discussion of column charts, and the design principles that apply to them, by creating a simple clustered column chart to display patient satisfaction scores collected on four outpatient clinics, as presented in Table 4.1. You'll see in this process that while it's easy to create a simple column chart, it's not easy to get it right the first time.

Table 4.1. Hypothetical Satisfaction Scores for Four Outpatient Clinics

Outpatient Clinic Satisfaction–FY12 Target = 82%	
Clinic	Satisfaction Score
East	82
Baker	74
Central	88
Howe	81

HOW-TO. If you create your own Excel charts, you might want to create this chart on your computer since we will be demonstrating how to modify it in the next chapter.

Open a blank slide in PowerPoint and click on the Insert tab in the ribbon. Select Chart and a dropdown box will appear with multiple chart options. The first variation of Column Chart (Clustered Column) will be highlighted; click OK. A split screen will appear with a sample chart on the left and an Excel spreadsheet with the sample labels and data on the right. The sample data consist of four rows (categories) and three columns (series).

Since we have only one series of data, click on the blue triangle in the lower right corner of the blue-highlighted data area in the spreadsheet and drag it to the left, so that the area enclosed by the blue box now includes four rows but only two columns (one for the category name and one for a single series of values). Delete the sample data for the other series (Series 2 and Series 3).

On the Excel spreadsheet, replace the category names (Category 1, Category 2, ...) with the clinic names (East, Baker, Central, and Howe). Change the "Series 1" label to "Satisfaction" and enter the satisfaction scores in their respective rows. Close the spreadsheet on the right side of the screen so that only the chart view is visible.

If you entered the data in Table 4.1 as described above, here's the resulting clustered column chart (Fig. 4.1).

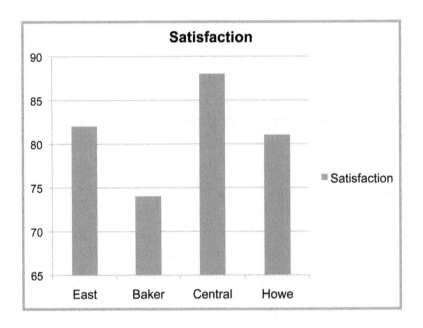

Fig. 4.1. Default Clustered Column Chart

Seem pretty good to you? There are actually three things wrong with this chart, one of them very seriously wrong. Can you identify them?

The first and most obvious problem in Fig. 4.1 is the presence of a legend, "Satisfaction," on the right side of the chart. Legends are used to identify different series of data. For example, if the chart contained data on satisfaction scores for each clinic for both 2011 and 2012 with a color code for 2011 and 2012 columns, you would need a legend to present that color code. Since this chart has only one series of data, there is no need for a legend.

Second, notice in Fig. 4.1 that the satisfaction score for the Baker clinic appears to be less than half the score of the Central clinic. Yet, the score for Baker is actually 84% of the score for Central and not less than half as it appears in the chart (Table 4.1: Baker, 74; Central, 88). The visual distortion in the chart is due to the fact that the low end of the y-axis has been truncated at a value of 65.

Excel automatically determines both the minimum and maximum values for the y-axis (i.e., the value axis) based on the data entered. If the range between the high and low values in the data-set is less than 20%, Excel's default setting automatically truncates the minimum value for the y-axis scale. In this instance, the range between the highest and lowest scores is less than 20% [(88 – 74)/74 = 19%)], resulting in the low end of the y-axis being truncated at a score of 65.

The rule for column (and bar) charts is that you should never truncate the low end of the value axis (in this case the y-axis). If you truncate the value axis of a column (or bar) chart, you get an erroneous visual impression of the differences between categories, since your focus is on the comparative lengths of the respective columns or bars. In a column (or bar) chart, the value axis should *always* start at zero even if the range of values is far from zero. Few (2009) goes so far as to recommend that software designers make it difficult or impossible to remove zero from the quantitative scale of a column or bar chart. We'll address how to manually set desired minimum and maximum scale values (i.e., override the Auto scale feature and enter fixed values for each) in Chapter 5.

HOW-TO. If you've created this chart on your computer and want to see how the Auto scale feature works, right click on the chart and select Edit Data (the spreadsheet with the data will appear). Change the score for Central from 88 to 96 and note what happens. You'll observe that the y-axis is no longer trun-cated at the low end (since the difference between high and low values is greater than 20%). However, you'll also note that the Auto scale feature has automatically increased the y-axis maxi-mum from 100% to 120%. Your boss will surely be pleased to see that you are aiming to have 120% of your patients satisfied! If you've ever seen or produced a chart where the high end of the value axis makes no sense, the Auto scale feature is the most likely culprit.

The third problem with Fig. 4.1 is that it has skinny columns. If your experience is similar to mine, you've seen many charts with skinny columns, since it's the Excel default setting. There's nothing technically wrong with skinny columns, but they are not aesthetically pleasing, and the empty space between them results in an unnecessary amount of chart space being devoted to noninformation. The rule of thumb is that the width of the columns or bars should be wider than the space separating them. Wong (2010) suggests that the width of the columns or bars should be about twice the width of the space between them and that seems to be a good choice.

OK, we've identified three things wrong with the chart originally generated by Excel:

1. The legend was unnecessary and should be eliminated.

2. The y-axis was truncated.

3. The columns were skinny; their width was less than the gap between them.

Figure 4.2 presents a well-designed clustered column chart of the data in Table 4.1. The three issues identified above have been addressed (legend eliminated, y-axis scale corrected, and columns increased in width). In addition, a number of other elements have been modified or added. The title has been modified to make it more informative. Data labels and a y-axis title have been added. Finally, a reference line showing the target value has been inserted, along with a legend.

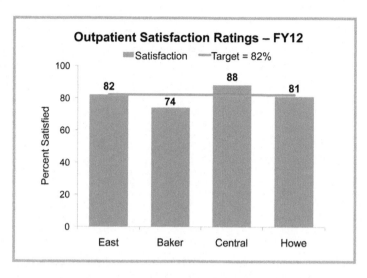

Fig. 4.2. Final Chart With Legend and Target Line

If you feel there is no need for a specific item in a legend (e.g. "Satisfaction" in Fig. 4.2), click on the legend (the entire legend will be highlighted). Then click on the portion of the legend you want to eliminate and hit the Delete key. This part of the legend will be deleted.

Chapter 5 will demonstrate how easy it is to get from Fig. 4.1 to Fig. 4.2 using the chart formatting options in Excel.

Using a Column Chart to Show a Trend Over Time

Fig. 4.3, which uses a column chart to show a trend over time, is clear and quite effective. However, using column charts to show trends over long time intervals is problematic. You'll find that when you look at a column chart that tracks performance over a long period of time, you are mentally tracing an imaginary line along the tops of the columns to discern the trend. Line charts do a much better job of showing trends over long time periods. Jelen (2011) suggests a cutoff of 12 time intervals for column charts over time. I prefer a cutoff of eight time intervals, because I can see the trend at a glance; with a larger number of time intervals, I find myself drawing that imaginary line in my head.

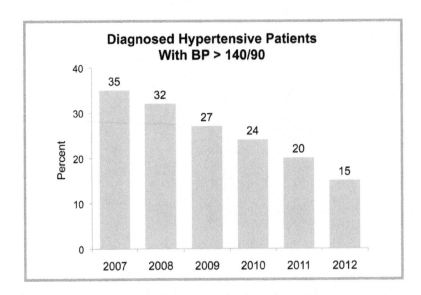

Fig. 4.3. Column Chart to Show Trend Over Time

If you are considering using a column chart to compare trends over a long time period for several different series, don't even think about it (Fig. 4.4).

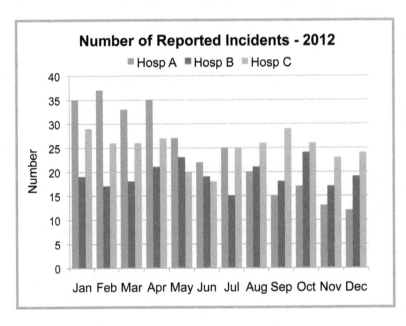

Fig. 4.4. Column Chart of Trends Over Time for Multiple Series

Stacked and 100% Stacked Column Charts

As indicated above, in a clustered column chart, the values for each series are represented by columns clustered next to each other for each x-axis category. In a stacked column chart, the values for each series are stacked on top of each other. Hence, for each x-axis category the values for the second series are placed on top of the value for the first series, and the values for each successive series are placed on top of the previous series in that category. The total height of the resulting cumulative column for that category represents the cumulative total of the values for all series in that category.

In a 100% stacked column chart, the values for each series are converted to percentages of the whole, and these percentages are stacked one upon the other, with the total height of the column equaling 100%. Examples of clustered, stacked, and 100% stacked columns using the same data are presented in Fig. 4.5.

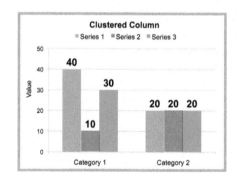

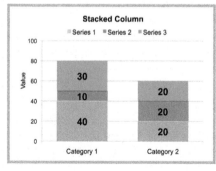
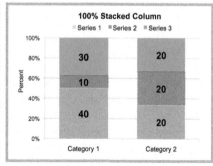

Fig. 4.5. Examples of Clustered, Stacked, and 100% Stacked Column Charts

> **TIP**
>
> When you enter raw scores to create a 100% stacked column chart, the data labels will be raw score values, not percentages. If you want to display data labels as percentages, calculate the percentages from the raw scores and create the 100% stacked chart by entering these percentages instead of raw scores. The graphic will look the same but data labels will now be percentages.

An Application

To illustrate the use of stacked and 100% stacked column charts, let's take a look at an example involving the use of palliative care services (PCS) in an intensive care unit (ICU). Table 4.2 presents data from a hypothetical quality improvement project with the goal of increasing PCS referrals on an ICU unit. These data include only ICU patients for whom PCS would be appropriate.

Table 4.2. Hypothetical Data on Palliative Care Service (PCS) Referrals in an ICU

ICU Patients Appropriate for Palliative Care Services (PCS)				
GOAL: To increase PCS referrals				
	A	B	C	D
Month	# Patients with PCS Referral	# Patients without PCS Referral	Total # of ICU Patients	% Patients with PCS Referral
October	3	3	6	50%
November	3	2	5	60%
December	2	7	9	22%
January	3	1	4	75%
February	2	1	3	67%
March	3	1	4	75%

There are a variety of ways in which charts can be used to display these data, with the goal of telling the story in the most effective way.

Clustered Column Chart: Number of PCS Referrals

Figure 4.6 is a clustered column chart showing the *number* of patients referred for PCS (column A in Table 4.2).

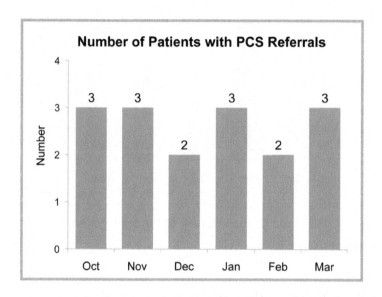

Fig. 4.6. Clustered Column Chart of Number of PCS Referrals

It appears from this chart that PCS referrals are not increasing. *That's not good.* However, suppose that the team was trying to increase referrals, but the number of patients appropriate for PCS has decreased. Perhaps the percentage of patients referred is a better way to display these data.

Clustered Column Chart: Percent Patients Referred

Figure 4.7 is a clustered column chart of the percentage of patients referred for PCS (column D in Table 4.2). It appears from this chart that the percentage of referrals has noticeably increased. *That's good.*

I remember one instance in which quarterly performance for four of five hospitals on an acute myocardial infarction (AMI) measure had a range of between 74 and 86%, while one hospital had achieved a remarkable 100%. The high-performing hospital was a rural hospital that had admitted only one AMI patient in the quarter, and they did exactly what they were supposed to do with that one case.

TIP

Whenever percentages based on very small sample sizes are presented in a chart, an indication of the sample sizes should be included in the chart (e.g., with the use of text boxes).

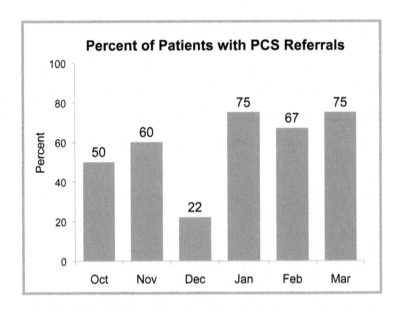

Fig. 4.7. Clustered Column Chart of Percent Patients Referred for PCS

As an aside, be cautious about percentages. Percentages can fluctuate wildly if based on small samples. If you see a chart with many exact percentages of 25%, 50%, 75%, and 100%, be suspicious that there may be only four cases. Similarly, exact percentages of 33% and 66% suggest samples of three cases, while exact percentages of 20%, 40%, 60%, 80% suggest samples of five cases.

Clustered Column Chart: Number of PCS Referrals and Total Number of Patients

You would draw two completely different conclusions from Figs. 4.6 and 4.7. Perhaps a chart showing both the number referred and the total number of patients would provide some clarification of this apparent discrepancy in performance.

Figure 4.8 is a clustered column chart showing both the number of patients referred and the total number of patients (columns A and C in Table 4.2).

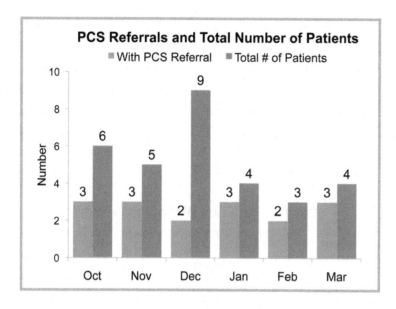

Fig. 4.8. Clustered Column Chart of Patients with PCS Referral and Total Number of Patients

This chart helps to clarify the contradictory conclusions of the two previous charts. It appears that the percentage of PCS referrals improved, not because the number of PCS referrals increased, but rather because the number of patients decreased. This chart presents a much more accurate picture than the two previous charts. However, you have to calculate rough percentages or proportions in your head—mental gymnastics—to discern that the two PCS referrals in December had a different significance from the two PCS referrals in February, since there were more patients in December than in February. Here's where stacked charts come in.

Stacked Column Chart: Patients Referred and Patients Not Referred

Figure 4.9 was created by selecting a stacked column chart, the second option in the Excel charts menu for column charts. A stacked column chart stacks the values for the second series on top of the values for the first series. Both the number with PCS referrals (blue)

and the number without PCS referrals (maroon) are indicated (columns A and B in Table 4.2). The cumulative height of the column represents the total number of patients, both those who had a referral as well as those who didn't. For example, the column for October shows that there were three patients referred for PCS (blue segment) and three patients not referred for PCS (maroon segment)—a total of six patients in all.

TIP

This small hypothetical example was constructed to demonstrate how in certain limited circumstances a stacked column chart may be helpful. However, as we'll see at the end of this section, several authors discourage the use of stacked column and bar charts completely.

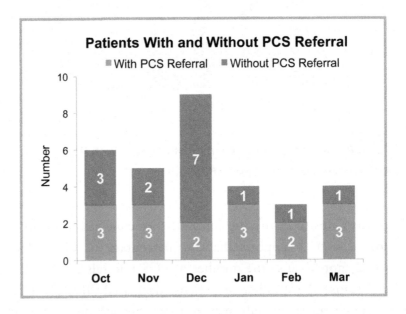

Fig. 4.9. Stacked Column Chart of Patients With and Without PCS Referral

Examining the chart in Fig. 4.9 leads to the same conclusion as Fig. 4.8, namely, that while the team seems to be doing better now, it appears that improvement is due to the decreased number of suitable patients rather than an increase in the number of referrals. The advantage of the stacked column chart is that it enables this to be perceived more quickly and more easily than in Fig. 4.8.

If you were the manager of this ICU, after seeing these data you would probably say something along the lines of, "Recently, the ICU is referring almost all patients who are appropriate, but I'd like to see what happens when we get a month with a greater number of appropriate patients. Does the team show an increase in the number of referrals, or does this remain at the two or three level?"

100% Stacked Column Chart: Patients Referred and Patients Not Referred

The 100% stacked column chart is the third option in the charts menu for column charts. Figure 4.10 is similar to the stacked column chart except that the data are expressed as percentages summing to 100%. The height of the column shows 100% of the patients; the length of the individual segments indicates the percentage contributed by each of the different series.

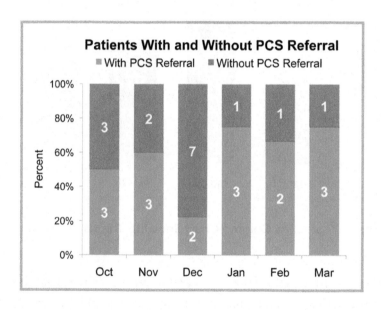

Fig. 4.10. 100% Stacked Column Chart of Patients With and Without PCS Referral

The conclusion drawn from this chart is similar to that drawn from the stacked column chart, except that it's not as immediately obvious that there were more suitable patients in December, since all the columns are the same height (100%). You have to mentally add the values of the two segments.

Use of Stacked Column Charts for More than Two Series of Data

Fig. 4.11 presents a stacked column chart of observation bed diagnoses for three groups over the course of four quarters.

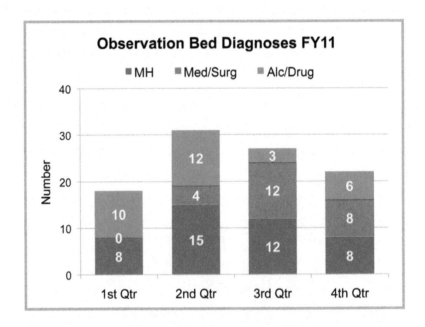

Fig. 4.11. Stacked Column Chart Showing Trends Over Time

Stacked column and 100% stacked column charts that include multiple series of data present a number of problems. First, it is difficult to compare the lengths of different segments when they don't have a common baseline (Few, 2004; Robbins, 2005; Wainer, 1997). Another problem is the confusion that occurs when one or another of the segments has a zero value (see Med/Surg for 1st Qtr in Fig. 4.11).

Because of these problems, Robbins (2005) recommends against using stacked column or bar charts. Others (Jones, 2007; Kosslyn,

2006) suggest that the segment with the least amount of change should be placed at the bottom so that other segments can be judged more accurately. If the most important information in a stacked column or bar chart is the change in one specific segment, and this change is difficult to follow because of changes in other segments, it is better to place this segment as the first series in the stacked column (so it has a common baseline). Other alternatives to stacked column charts with multiple series include creating separate column charts, one for each series, in a small multiple format as described in Chapter 3 or, where trends over time are involved, a line chart with multiple lines.

Histograms

A histogram is a column chart showing the distribution of data. Figure 4.12 shows the distribution of people with different body mass index (BMI) scores. Data are from a table of percentages in Van Wye et al. (2008). Separate columns are plotted in Fig. 4.12 but the space between them—known as the gap width—has been reduced to zero. Chapter 5 will show how this is done.

> **TIP**
>
> Comparing distributions of several groups can be done by comparing their respective histograms, but perhaps the best way is to compare box-and-whisker plots for each of the distributions. This type of chart is not included in Excel, though it is available in other software programs and can be created in Excel with some effort. Appendix E in Few (2012) shows how to create box plots in Excel.

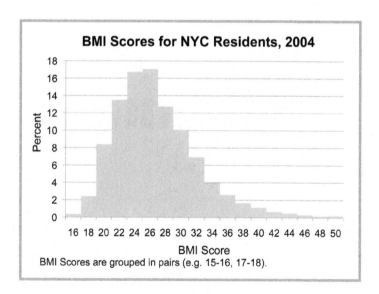

Fig. 4.12. Histogram of BMI Scores (Data source: Van Wye et al., 2008)

Pareto Charts

Pareto charts, a mainstay of many quality improvement initiatives, are charts of data with discrete categories on one axis with the columns (or bars) sorted in increasing or decreasing order of magnitude. It is named after the Italian engineer and economist Wilfredo Pareto, who in 1906 observed that 80% of the land in Italy was owned by 20% of the population. Pareto charts are often used in quality improvement initiatives to visualize which components contribute most to a particular problem. This helps to focus attention on the components that, when addressed, will yield the greatest improvement in outcome.

Figure 4.13 is a Pareto chart of overtime by ward, based on an actual quality improvement project.

I'm a fan of the Willie Sutton school of quality improvement. Willie was a famous bank robber who reportedly was asked in prison, "Why do you rob banks?" Willie's answer was direct and simple: "Because that's where the money is." As someone interested in quality improvement, you should always try to identify the critical components that, when improved, would result in the biggest bang for the buck.

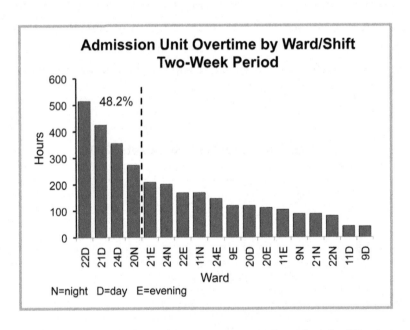

Fig. 4.13. Pareto Chart of Admission Unit Overtime by Ward and Shift

In Fig. 4.13, the order of the wards was determined by how much overtime each ward used during this two-week period (from highest to lowest) rather than by ward number. As you can see, this reorganization of the data is very helpful in identifying the wards with the highest overtime usage along with the cumulative percentage of overtime for which they accounted. In this case, four ward shifts (22% of the 18 ward shifts) accounted for 48.2% of the total overtime. This chart analysis suggests that the administration should focus on the overtime control processes of the four ward/shifts with the highest overtime.

HOW-TO. The dashed vertical line in Fig. 4.13 was added by Insert | Shapes | Line. Holding the Shift key down while drawing this line will ensure that it is a perfectly straight line. Once the line is drawn, right click on the line | Format Object | Format Shape | Line Style | Dash type | Dash. In this same menu, you can also change the width of this line. The percent for the four highest wards and key for night/day/evening were added as text boxes. This was accomplished by Insert | Text Box | type in the text and increasing the font as desired.

When inserting a text box or shape into a chart, be sure to have the chart area selected (frame highlighted) when inserting the material (e.g., Chart Tools|Layout|Insert). This will ensure that the additions will be embedded into the chart. If you insert materials into a chart without the chart area being highlighted, they will appear in the chart, but if you copy and paste the chart elsewhere (e.g., as a picture), the additions will not be included.

TIP

To determine whether an addition to a chart has been embedded, hold down the left mouse key and move the mouse to encompass an area which includes the chart. When you release the left mouse key, if only the chart area is highlighted all additions have been embedded. If some additions in the chart are also highlighted, they have not been embedded in the chart.

The customary presentation format for Pareto charts includes a cumulative percent line in addition to the columns. This requires a dual axis chart, which will be discussed in Chapter 6 (line charts). However, I have found that staff are often unfamiliar with cumulative percent lines, and this makes a Pareto chart containing this element more puzzling than it need be. I prefer to identify these break points with a dotted line and the percent contribution in a text box, as in Fig. 4.13. One or more of these break points can be highlighted depending on the shape of the data.

From one point of view, the strength of a Pareto chart is that it identifies areas that are key to solving a problem, in this case excessive overtime. But, from another and perhaps more important point of view, the strength of a Pareto chart is that it enables administrators or other problem solvers to leave the well-functioning areas alone.

Imagine if the administration had not done a Pareto analysis but instead assembled the supervisors of all 18 ward/shifts into a room and lectured them about the importance of controlling overtime, pointing out how poorly the facility was performing in this area. If you were the supervisor of one of the wards with low overtime usage, how would you feel? Unappreciated? Perhaps even angry that you had to be there? If the administration had used this blunderbuss approach to reducing overtime and, in the process, alienated only *half* of the 14 supervisors who were doing well controlling overtime, they would have alienated almost 40% (7 of 18) of all supervisors in the unit!

Bar Charts

Bar charts are similar in concept to column charts except for the fact that the bars are horizontal. Clustered bar, stacked bar, and 100% stacked bar charts can be used interchangeably with their respective column charts with a couple of exceptions.

Bar charts are especially useful when the x-axis labels are long. Jha, Perlin, Kizer, and Dudley (2003) presented a comparison between performance by the Veterans Health Administration (VHA) and the Medicare system for certain cardiac, diabetes, and pneumococcal performance measures. Figure 4.14, using data from the Jha et al. (2003) study (but not part of that article), demonstrates how lengthy x-axis labels affect a column chart.

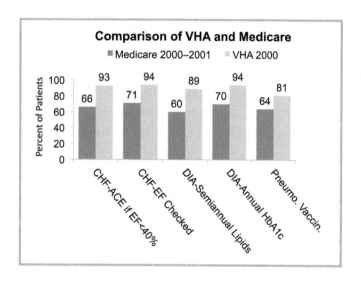

Fig. 4.14. Long X-Axis Labels in a Column Chart Format (Data source: Jha et al., 2003)

Since the x-axis labels are too long to fit horizontally across the x-axis, they are often slanted, with the result that reading them becomes difficult and the area devoted to the chart is reduced in size. The horizontal orientation of bar charts can help in this instance (Fig. 4.15).

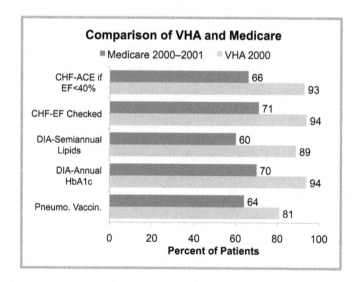

Fig. 4.15. Long X-Axis Labels in a Bar Chart Format (Data source: Jha et al., 2003)

Note how the category labels are much easier to read both as a result of their horizontal orientation and the ability to use two lines to accommodate the longer labels. In addition, there is much more room allotted to the chart plot area. The chart plot area in Fig. 4.15 is over 80% larger than the chart plot area in Fig. 4.14.

One area where bar charts should *not* be used is to show trends over time, even for short intervals. Most observers expect to see time conveyed from left to right. Asking observers to view a chart with time moving in a vertical direction (up or down) is perceptually awkward.

Dot Plots

Dot plots are used to present information on categorical data when the number of categories is large and, as a consequence, the use of multiple very thin columns or bars would appear cluttered (Robbins, 2005). Markers ("dots"), placed at the value for each category, take the place of columns or bars. In addition to simplifying the appearance of the chart, another advantage of dot plots is that the value axis can be truncated, since columns and bars are not involved.

Dot plots are usually portrayed in a horizontal (bar chart) format to enable the labeling of the various categories. Dot plots also frequently employ a Pareto format from highest to lowest or vice versa depending on the data. Figure 4.16 presents a dot plot of falls per 1,000 patient days for 14 nursing homes with the Burke nursing home highlighted.

Creating a dot plot with the category names on the vertical axis is not an option in Excel, but can be accomplished with some add-ons to Excel. However, if you have only an occasional need for a dot plot, it can easily be created in Excel if you are willing to do some hand work. The method that produced the chart in Fig. 4.16 is described in Appendix C.

Although dot charts can be used to show static differences among categorical elements, they present no data-over-time context for any of the categories in the chart. A small multiples (multipanel) display

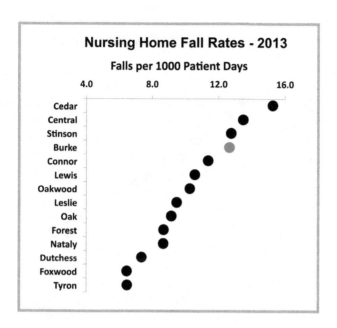

Fig. 4.16. Dot Plot With Category Labels on the Vertical Axis

of fall rates for each of the nursing homes over the 12 months of the year (using the same value axis range for each chart) would enable a more thorough exploration of differences in fall rates.

Balestracci (2009, pp. 131–135) uses a very dramatic illustration of the problem associated with using only aggregate summary statistics. He presents tabular data on the means and standard deviations of mortality rates for three hospitals over the course of 30 months. All three have similar means and standard deviations. Yet, despite the comparability of means and standard deviations, one hospital has a significant increasing trend over the course of the 30 months, one a significant decreasing trend, and one a stable but highly variable trend. Clearly, the aggregate data misrepresented the situation and would have led to an erroneous conclusion, namely, that all three hospitals had comparable and presumably stable mortality rates.

If the aim of the chart is to indicate where a particular facility appears among its peers *and the specific names of the peers are not important*, a simple line chart with markers may be used with the line deleted, as in Fig. 4.17.

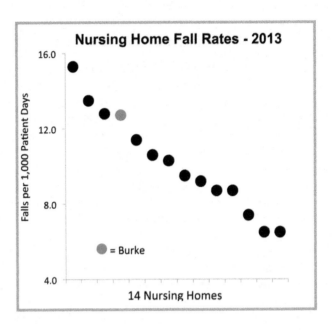

Fig. 4.17. Dot Plot Using a Line With Markers (Line Deleted)

TIP

If markers are too close together to select one over others nearby, open the datasheet, temporarily change the value for the data point of interest to separate it from the others in the chart, click on it in its changed position, change the format as desired, and reenter the correct value for this data point to place it back where it belongs.

HOW-TO. Figure 4.17 is a line chart with markers with the data sorted in descending order. The lines have been removed so that only the markers remain. Lines can be removed by double left clicking on the line | Format Data Series | Line Color | No Line.

The circle for Burke was highlighted by left clicking on the marker for Burke (all markers will be highlighted) and then left clicking again to highlight the marker for Burke only. Double left click on the highlighted Burke marker | Format Data Point | Marker Fill | Solid Fill | Red and Marker Line Color | Solid Line | Red.

The single legend for Burke was created by inserting a circle shape the same size as the markers in the chart, filling it with red color, and pairing it with a text box with the entry "= Burke."

Other Column and Bar Chart Variations

We have discussed the use of three variations of column charts (clustered, stacked, and 100% stacked) and three variations of bar charts (clustered, stacked, and 100% stacked). Each of these used rectangular shapes for the columns and bars. What about the 16 other versions of column charts and the 12 other versions of bar charts available in Excel and listed in Appendix A?

Seven of the additional column chart variations and three of the additional bar chart variations are labeled "3-D." We have already discussed why 3-D charts should not be used. That eliminates seven column and three bar chart variations from consideration.

All of the remaining column and bar chart variations employ shapes other than rectangles, specifically cylinders, cones, or pyramids. As illustrated in Appendix D, all variations involving cylinders, cones, or pyramids are pseudo 3-D charts. They are wolves in sheep's clothing and should be avoided. Thus, of the 34 variations of column and bar charts, we are left with only six—the six basic charts that we have discussed in this chapter.

SUMMARY

- Column and bar charts are very effective for conveying data on discrete categories. Bar charts are particularly useful when category labels are lengthy.

- Column charts can be used to display a trend over time but only for a limited number of time periods (preferably no more than 8). Bar charts should not be used for displaying trends over time.

- Stacked and 100% stacked column or bar charts are sometimes helpful in conveying information above and beyond that of clustered column or bar charts.

SUMMARY *(continued)*

- Histograms are useful for displaying distributions; Pareto charts are useful for identifying target areas for quality improvement activity.

- Dot plots allow the plotting of categorical data for a large number of categories that would make their display using columns or bars problematic. Dot plots are often presented in Pareto format.

- Of the 34 variations of column and bar charts available in Excel, only six convey information quickly and easily for most observers: column charts with rectangular shapes (clustered, stacked, and 100% stacked) and the bar charts with rectangular shapes (clustered, stacked, and 100% stacked). All other Excel variations of column or bar charts are either 3-D charts (labeled as such) or are pseudo 3-D charts and should be avoided.

Changing the Format
of Chart Elements

In addition to chart type and variation, there are multiple ways to modify individual elements within a chart (title, axis titles, axis labels, legend, data labels, color scheme, etc.). Jelen (2011) indicates that there are 780 quadrillion ways to configure a chart in Excel. This chapter will introduce chart formatting and demonstrate how easy this process can be, highlighting two ways to access chart format options: chart tools and shortcuts.

Chart Tools

Whenever you click on a chart, either in PowerPoint or in an Excel spreadsheet, three Chart Tool tabs appear on the ribbon. These Chart Tool tabs are labeled Design, Layout, and Format, and they access the major chart format options, such as adding a title, axis titles, or a legend to a chart. Anyone who will be creating their own charts should be familiar with these tabs. An overview of the options available through these tabs is presented in Appendix E.

Shortcuts

A number of shortcuts can also be used to modify charts. Two of the most useful shortcuts are (a) a double left click on a chart element and (b) a single right click on a chart element.

Double Left Click

If you double left click on a chart element, it will bring up a menu of Format options for that element. For example, if you double left click on the x-axis labels, a Format Axis box will appear with options for the x-axis. The options are different for each of the elements in a chart and are too extensive to be covered here. The best way to become familiar with them is to use them in practice.

Single Right Click

If you single right click on a chart element, it will bring up a mini toolbar and a menu. The mini toolbar enables you to change the font (type, size, color, attributes) as well as fill and outline color for this chart element. If you right click on the chart border, you can change the font characteristics for all text in the chart. The accompanying menu allows other changes to be made, some specific to the element selected and some more general like changing the chart type and editing the data.

Column Chart Example

We'll show how easy it is to change the format of chart elements by using some of these methods to correct the problems identified in the default column chart of clinic satisfaction created in Chapter 4. Figure 5.1 is the original chart we created. As you may recall, there were three problems with this chart.

TIP

If you want to see what options are available with the Format Options box for each of the various elements in a chart, double left click on any chart element (e.g., x-axis labels). When the Format options box for that element appears, move it to the side so that you can see both the chart and the options box. Then click on each chart element in the chart and the Format Options box will change to the one specific for that element.

TIP

In the upper right hand corner of the mini toolbar there is a drop down box that will allow you to apply the mini toolbar effects to different elements in the chart. This is yet another way to highlight a specific chart element; an identical drop down box appears on the left side of the Chart Tools Layout tab.

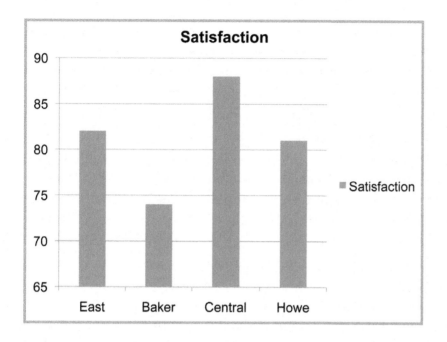

Fig. 5.1. Original Clinic Satisfaction Chart

The legend is unnecessary and should be eliminated. Left click on the legend to highlight it and hit Delete on the keyboard. Done! When you do this, notice how the chart plot area expanded to take up the space formerly occupied by the legend. This is the reason why it is better to position the legend above or below the chart or even within the chart itself, if space allows. (Eliminating the legend could also have been accomplished by using the Layout tab of the Chart Tools: Layout | Legend | None.)

The y-axis was truncated, but the y-axis should never be truncated in a column (or bar) chart. Double left click on the y-axis labels, and a Format Axis box will appear with Axis Options highlighted. The top section will have options for the Minimum, Maximum, Major unit, and Minor unit. You will note that the radio button for Auto is checked for each. As indicated previously, Auto scale allows the Excel software to determine the maximum and minimum values for the value axis (the y-axis in this case) automatically, based on the data entered.

IN PRACTICE

There is no one right way to access the format options in Excel; indeed there are multiple ways. What I describe are the methods that work best for me. In time you will adopt your own preferred ways.

In our satisfaction example, this led to an automatic truncation at the low end of the y-axis, resulting in a minimum value of 65. To correct this, click on the Fixed radio button for Minimum, and change the minimum value in the adjacent box from 65.0 to 0.0. The automatic feature also resulted in a maximum of 90. Since these are percent satisfied scores, you probably would prefer to have the maximum set at 100. If so, click on the Fixed radio button for Maximum and change the maximum value from 90.0 to 100.0.

In this same area you can also determine the Major unit (interval) for the y-axis values. With the truncated axis, this was automatically set at 5. When you changed the range of the y-axis scale to 0 to 100, the gridline interval automatically changed to 20. You can change it to any interval you want by clicking on the Fixed radio button for Major unit and entering the desired value.

The columns were skinny. Double left click on any column and a Format Data Series box will appear with Series Options highlighted. The second Series Option is Gap Width. As you can see, it is automatically set at 150%, meaning that the default gap between columns in this chart is 1.5 times the width of the columns—the opposite of what you want, since the gap width should be about half the width of the columns (i.e., around 50%). Move the Gap Width slider bar down from 150% to 50% or thereabouts. When you release the slider bar, you will see the gap width change, and can adjust it further if necessary.

A few other changes. While we're at it, we might as well make a few other changes to improve our chart. Let's add data labels to the tops of each column to make the actual values clear. To add data labels, right click on any column. In the menu, select Add Data Labels, and the labels will be inserted for this series. If you add data labels to a chart, and they are partially obscured by other elements in the chart, left click on the problematic label. This will highlight all labels in this series. Left click on the problematic label again, and only this label will be highlighted. Drag it with the mouse to adjust its position.

TIP

If you have data labels, do you still need value axis labels? Technically, no since you can read the data values directly. However, I always find it reassuring to see the value axis labels to know for certain whether the value axis scale has been truncated.

Since data labels have been added, there is no need for gridlines. Left click on one of the gridlines (other than the top gridline, which is actually the plot area border). All gridlines will be highlighted. Hit the Delete key and the gridlines will be deleted. Alternatively, you can click on the chart | Layout | Gridlines | Primary Horizontal Gridlines | None.

Figure 5.2 presents the modified chart with the legend eliminated, a y-axis with a range of 0 to 100, a y-axis interval of 20, a reduced gap width between columns, the addition of data labels, and the removal of gridlines.

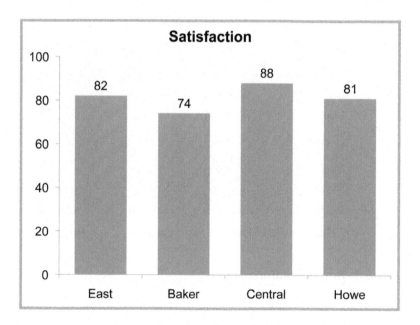

Fig. 5.2. Clustered Column Chart With Modifications

Ok, that looks better. Now go back to the original data in Table 4.1. Is there any additional information in Table 4.1 that you might want to include in the chart?

What about the 82% target value? It would seem important to indicate in the chart how well each of the wards was performing in relation to this target. As Few (2009) points out, "anything that makes comparisons easier, such as including reference lines or

TIP

I often put the actual value of the target in the spreadsheet label above the data so that this value will appear in the legend along with the series label. This obviates the need for viewers to guess at the target value, especially when it is a value between major value axis intervals.

reference regions, is worth doing" (p. 96). Let's add the target value to our chart.

Right click on the chart border and select Edit Data to bring up the spreadsheet of data. We'll use the third column on the spreadsheet (column C) to enter the target values. In cell C1, enter "Target = 82%." Then in the row for each ward, enter "82," the target value. Your chart should now look like Fig. 5.3.

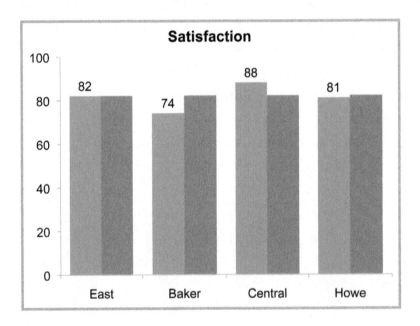

Fig. 5.3. Target Columns Added

The target data are there, but we've created two new problems. First, you need a legend since there are now two series of data. Second, our chart doesn't look very elegant (to say the least) with the target columns adjacent to each of our satisfaction score columns. Let's see what we can do.

Adding a legend. Click on the chart | Layout tab | Legend | Show Legend at Top. The legend will appear at the top of the chart. Since we entered the actual target value in the heading for satisfaction scores on our spreadsheet, the target value will appear as part of the legend.

Changing target columns to a line. In performance charts such as this, targets often appear as lines. Let's convert our target columns to a line. Right click on any target column. Each of the target columns will be highlighted and a box of options will appear. Select Change Series Chart Type, and the Change Chart Type menu will appear. Select Line, and then the first variation (Line, with no markers), and click OK. In this step you are telling the software that you want this series of data, the target data, to be plotted as a line without markers rather than a column. The target line will appear as a line across your chart, making it easy to see which wards have met the target and which have not.

Changing the color of the target line. Usually target lines are green. If you want to change this target line to green (or any other color) or increase its thickness, double left click on the target line and the Format Data Series menu will appear. Click on Line Color to change the color of the line and on Line Styles to change the thickness of the line. A description of the color palette available in Excel and how to replicate any color is presented in Appendix F.

Charts with both columns and lines can be used for a variety of purposes other than for showing level of performance and a target value, for example, actual budget expenditure (column) versus base budget adjusted for inflation (line), or staff positions filled (column) versus staff positions authorized (line). If you want to create a chart composed of variables that require different y-axis values (e.g., change in budget dollars in millions and change in number of filled positions in thousands), you will need a dual y-axis chart. This type of chart will be described in Chapter 6 (line charts).

Adding a chart title. Click on the chart | Layout tab | Chart Title | Above Chart. A text box with Chart Title will appear. You can enter the title you choose in this box. In this instance, we'll enter "Outpatient Satisfaction Ratings—FY12."

Adding a y-axis title. Click on the chart | Layout | Axis Titles | Primary Vertical Axis Title | Rotated Title. A text box with Axis Title will appear to the left of the y-axis labels. You can insert the title you choose in this box. In this instance, we'll enter "Percent Satisfied."

Figure 5.5 presents the final version of our chart.

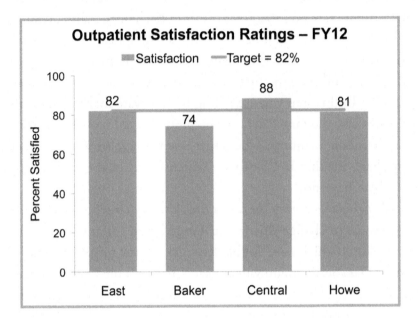

Fig. 5.4. Final Chart With Legend and Target Line

Now that you have modified your chart to your satisfaction, you can save it as a template to use in the future for other data sets. Click on the chart | Design | Save as Template | insert file name | Save. In selecting a file name, it is helpful to choose one that describes the template. For example, in the case above, a file name such as "Outpt Satis-Blue Columns" would be preferable to a generic name such as "Template 1." When you want to use this same format for another set of data, select Insert Chart | Templates (the category above Column charts), and a listing of all the templates you have saved will appear. Select the one you want.

SUMMARY

Changing the format of charts is not difficult. The same procedures used to change the format of a column chart in this chapter, or very similar procedures, can be used with other chart types. Though the procedures may initially seem somewhat complex, as you use these techniques, they will become familiar to you and much easier to use.

6

Displaying Trends: Line Charts

- The design of line charts to accurately portray trends in data

- Dual axis charts and cautions in their use

- Problems with stacked and 100% stacked line charts

- Run charts: what they are and how to interpret them

- Data exploration with line charts

The primary purpose of a line chart is to show a trend over time (e.g., minutes, days, weeks) or across any x-axis categories that have a sequence base (e.g., consecutive admissions, successive batches). While column charts may be used to display a trend over a short number of intervals, line charts are suitable for either short- or long-time periods or sequences. Lines can be drawn either with or without markers at the individual data points.

Lines should not be used to connect values for discrete x-axis categories (i.e. those whose placement along the x-axis has no time or sequence base). This applies even to numerical designations for discrete categories, like Wards 107, 108, 109, 110. These can be listed in numerical sequence, but their accompanying values should not be connected with lines. Columns or bars should be used to display data on discrete categories.

An Application

You're a member of a team on a unit that treats patients admitted with acute myocardial infarctions (AMIs). One of the initial treatments for these patients is to receive thrombolytic drug therapy. This process is time-sensitive because the patient's prognosis is much better if this therapy is given shortly after admission. You have a goal of 30 minutes from admission to administer thrombolytic therapy, referred to as door-to-needle time. However, your unit has not been meeting this goal.

In order to improve this process, you collect data on the next 15 AMI admissions (door-to-needle times and the reasons for delay). Then, over the course of a couple of weeks, you introduce a number of process changes to address the major reasons for delay. After the process changes have been introduced, you collect door-to-needle times for the next 15 AMI admissions. A study along similar lines was conducted by Bonetti et al. (2000).

Table 6.1 presents the hypothetical data collected on these 30 patients (15 pre-intervention and 15 post-intervention patients).

Table 6.1. Hypothetical Door-to-Needle Time for
Thrombolysis for Successive Patients

Pre-Intervention		Post-Intervention	
Patient	Time (min)	Patient	Time (min)
1	54	1	47
2	37	2	56
3	28	3	42
4	84	4	32
5	76	5	36
6	37	6	27
7	49	7	35
8	53	8	46
9	26	9	32
10	67	10	41
11	104	11	48
12	29	12	46
13	48	13	25
14	83	14	37
15	89	15	29

Figure 6.1 presents a line chart of these data with an indication
of when interventions were implemented. Note that the connecting
line between the 15th patient in the pre-intervention phase and the
first patient in the post-intervention phase has been omitted since
a two-week period elapsed during which the interventions were
implemented.

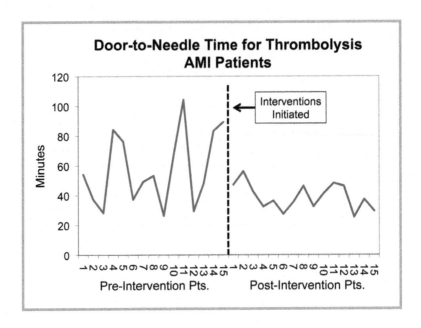

Fig. 6.1. Door-to-Needle Time for AMI Patients

The pattern in Fig. 6.1 seems clear: a decline in door-to-needle time after the interventions were introduced. Whether this change represents a real change in the process or is merely reflective of the natural variation in the process will be discussed later in this chapter.

HOW-TO. The dashed vertical line was added by Insert | Shapes | Line. Holding the Shift key down while drawing this line will ensure that it is a perfectly straight line. Once the line is drawn, right click on the line | Format Object | Format Shape | Line Style | Dash Type | Dash. The notation "Interventions Initiated" was added by Insert | Text Box | type in the desired text.

Again, just a reminder to be sure to have the chart area selected (frame highlighted) when inserting the material (text box, shapes, etc.). This will ensure that the additions will be embedded into the chart and, if the chart is copied, they will be copied along with the chart. If you insert materials using the

Layout tab of the Chart Tools, the material will automatically be imbedded in the chart. They will not be imbedded if you use the Insert tab and the chart is not highlighted when you make the insertion.

Eliminating the line between the last patient of the pre-intervention phase and the first patient of the post-intervention phase was achieved by left clicking on the line segment to be removed (all data points highlighted) | left click again on the line segment to be removed. Right click on this line segment | Format Data Point (in the menu) | Line Color | No Line. Just this segment of the line will be eliminated.

Truncation

In contrast to column and bar charts, the y-axis in line charts may be truncated at whatever value seems reasonable—keeping in mind, of course, that the more you truncate it, the greater the differences will appear among the plotted values. Use your judgment. You don't want it to appear as if there was a huge decline when the value went from 87 to 84 on a scale of 0 to 100, especially if this difference is well within the normal variability of the process. Also note that if the goal is at a certain level, you probably would not want to truncate the scale to the extent that you exclude this value from the y-axis range.

Trend Lines

Excel allows you to easily insert trend lines into a line chart. If there is more than one series in your line chart, separate trend lines can be displayed for each series. To prevent confusion, it would be helpful to color the trend lines in the same color as their respective data points. How to insert and interpret trend lines will be covered in Chapter 8 (scatter charts).

Balestracci (2009) cautions against the automatic use of trend lines, noting that they are far too frequently used and often lead to conclusions that are either totally inaccurate or misleading. Your decision on whether or not to add a trend line should be based on a visual inspection of the pattern *prior* to adding a trend line.

Unequal Time Intervals

Sometimes data are collected on a time-as-available basis, resulting in data at unequal time intervals, as in Table 6.2.

Table 6.2. Data Collected at Unequal Time Intervals

Date	Value
1/1/12	4
1/14/12	5
1/31/12	2
4/1/12	3
6/2/12	5

To show an accurate representation of a trend over time when data collection occurs at irregular intervals, the x-axis should be spaced as a calendar would (i.e., including x-axis intervals for periods for which no data were collected). Thus, the chart of the data in Table 6.2 should show February, March, and May on the x-axis, even though no data were collected during these months.

If unequal time intervals are displayed as equal time intervals (i.e., as text), a different and erroneous picture of the trend over time will emerge (Jelen, 2011; Robbins, 2005). In the data in Table 6.2, three of the five measures were obtained in the first month of this five-month period. The chart on the left of Fig. 6.2, with a date-based x-axis, correctly displays the early decline in this five-month period (placing the data points exactly where they belong, even mid-month). The chart on the right in Fig. 6.2, with a text-based x-axis (i.e., equally spaced x-axis intervals) gives the erroneous impression that the decline occurred in the middle of this five-month period.

If data are entered in the form of month/day/year, Excel will automatically display the appropriate date scale axis, spacing the categories as they would appear on a calendar. However, Jelen (2011)

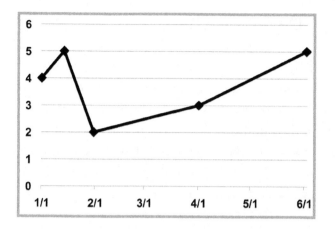 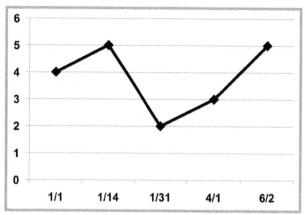

Fig. 6.2. Date-Spaced Scale Versus Equal-Spaced Scale

cautions that you should always check to be sure that this happens. He notes, for example, that if just numeric years are entered (e.g., 2008, 2009, 2011), Excel will consider this a text category, and the year 2010 will not appear on the x-axis.

HOW-TO. If you want to change equal time intervals (i.e., text format) to unequal time intervals (i.e., calendar format), double left click on the x-axis | Format Axis | Axis Type | Date Axis. Since a line drawn between irregularly spaced points suggests a specific pattern between these points, you might want to consider using just the markers without a connecting line.

Sometimes (e.g., in tracking performance over time) the information of interest might be the overall trend and the specific value of the last data point. In this case, create a line chart without data labels. Left click on the last data point (all data points will be highlighted); left click again on the last data point, and only that data point will be highlighted. Right click on this last data point | Add Data Label. The data label for the last data point will be added.

If you want to see how the equal and unequal time intervals work in practice, insert a line chart with markers into a PowerPoint slide. Change the category names to 2007, 2008, 2010, and 2011; leave the sample data alone. Expand the slide view | double left click on the x-axis | Format Axis | and in the Axis Type toggle back and forth between Text axis and Date axis. Note how the x-axis in the chart changes.

Deviation Charts

A deviation chart displays differences (values or percentages) between a series of data points and a reference line at zero (Harris, 1999). This requires plotting negative numbers, and as a result the value "0" appears somewhere in the middle of the y-axis. If you create either a line or column deviation chart, the x-axis and its labels automatically cross at the zero point, and the line or columns may run through the x-axis labels, sometimes making them difficult to read (Fig. 6.3).

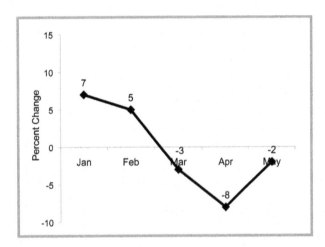 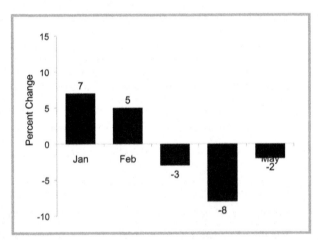

Fig. 6.3. Charts With Zero in the Middle of the Y-Axis

Appendix G shows how to format a deviation chart so that the x-axis labels appear at the bottom of the chart.

Dual Axes

Sometimes you may want to visually compare trends for two series of data that are on completely different scales. In this case, one option is to use a dual axis chart, that is, a chart with a secondary y-axis. Table 6.3 presents VHA data on the number of inpatient admissions (in thousands) and the number of outpatient visits (in millions) from 1995 to 2003. Data are estimated based on a chart that appeared in Perlin, Kolodnor, & Roswell (2004).

Table 6.3. Veterans Health Administration: Inpatient Admissions and Outpatient Visits (Data source: Perlin et al., 2004)

	Veterans Health Administration								
	1995	1996	1997	1998	1999	2000	2001	2002	2003
Inpatient Admissions (thousands)	900	825	745	660	610	595	585	590	595
Outpatient Visits (millions)	27	28	32	33	35	41	45	47	51

If you were to plot these data on a chart with a single y-axis with a maximum of 60 million (to accommodate the 51 million outpatient visits in 2003), as in Fig. 6.4, the inpatient admissions (expressed in thousands) would barely show a change, even though they decreased 34%, from 900,000 in 1995 to 595,000 in 2003.

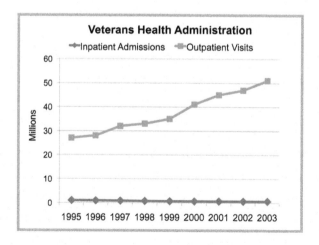

Fig. 6.4. Veterans Health Administration Data: Single Y-Axis Chart

To more accurately show the trends in each measure, one solution is to create separate charts, one for inpatient admissions and one for outpatient visits. Another solution is to create a dual axis chart. In a dual axis chart, each series of data is plotted on a different y-axis, one on the left and one on the right, as in Fig. 6.5. The truncations for the y-axes were chosen to cover the range of the respective data, as in Perlin et al. (2004). In order to ensure that a link is made between a plotted line and the appropriate y-axis for that line, the y-axis lines were made thicker and their colors changed to the respective colors of the lines.

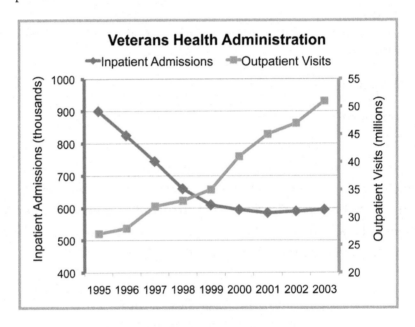

Fig. 6.5. Veterans Health Administration Data: Dual Axis Chart (Perlin et al., 2004, redrawn with permission)

HOW-TO. Plotting one data series on a secondary axis is very simple. Double left click on the data series you want to change to a second vertical axis | Format Data Series | Series Options | Secondary Axis. You can create dual axis charts with both series as lines or one series as a line and the other as a column. Keep in mind, however, that if one series is a column in a dual axis chart, you cannot truncate the y-axis for this series.

Changing the thickness and color of the respective axis lines is done by double left clicking on the axis | Format Axis | Line Color | Solid Line (to change the color of line) | Line Style (to change the thickness of the line). You can also change the color of the axis values and the axis title as well, if you desire, by right clicking on them and using the mini toolbar.

TIP

If the chart is to be printed in black and white, the two lines can be differentiated by solid and dashed lines. Connection to the appropriate y-axis can be enhanced by including solid and dashed lines adjacent to their respective y-axis titles.

Keep in mind that the visual relationship between the two variables in a dual axis chart can easily be changed, even dramatically so, by modifying the range of either one or both of the y-axis scales. Trends could appear quite different solely depending on the range chosen for the respective y-axis scales. When either viewing or constructing a dual axis chart, the first thing to which you should direct your attention is the range of values chosen for each of the y-axis scales.

Few (2004) originally felt that dual axis charts had a role to play in communicating information, but he's since had second thoughts on this. "Today, I can't think of a single case where there isn't a better solution than a graph with a dual-scaled axis" (Few, 2008, p. 1). His concerns are that in dual axis charts, viewers are tempted to draw magnitude comparisons between the two series and to give meaning to any intersections that might occur. Both of these features (relative magnitude and intersects) are meaningless, since they are dependent on the y-axis scales chosen for each series.

Because of these concerns, Few (2008) recommends either creating separate charts for the two series or plotting percent differences from a common baseline (e.g., the starting value for each variable) on a single y-axis. Figure 6.6 presents a chart of the VHA data plotted as percent differences from the 1995 baseline.

TIP

If you are creating a line chart with many lines and/ or long series names, placing the series names adjacent to their respective lines and eliminating the legend may be the best option, if the pattern of lines allows for this. The series names can be inserted with text boxes.

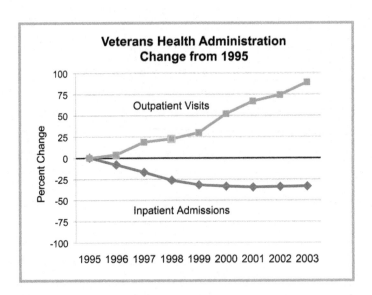

Fig. 6.6. Veterans Health Administration: Single Axis Chart of Percent Differences From Baseline

The information in the chart in Fig. 6.6 is the same as the information conveyed by Perlin et al. (2004), namely, that while inpatient admissions were declining, outpatient visits were increasing. However, in contrast to the dual axis chart (Fig. 6.5), there is no visual impression that the magnitude of these changes was similar or that there was anything unique about the intersection of lines that occurred between 1998 and 1999. An advantage of the dual axis chart showing percent differences from baseline, over presenting these data in two separate charts, is that it allows an immediate visual comparison of the percentage changes between the two variables at different points in time. Creating two separate charts would require the observer to move back and forth between the charts to make comparisons at different time points.

Because of the problems in the interpretation of dual axis charts, Wainer (1997) writes ominously, "The use of a pie chart is sinful, but the sin is venial. The sin of a 'double Y-axis graph' is mortal. If there is a just God, I'm sure that there is a special place in the inferno reserved for its perpetrators" (p. 91).

If you intend to create a dual axis chart, say some prayers first.

Stacked Line Charts

Figure 6.7 presents a simple line chart of overtime hours per month for three wards over the course of four years. The patterns of these data are quite clear: Ward A shows an increasing trend, Ward B shows a decreasing trend, and Ward C remains constant over the four-year period.

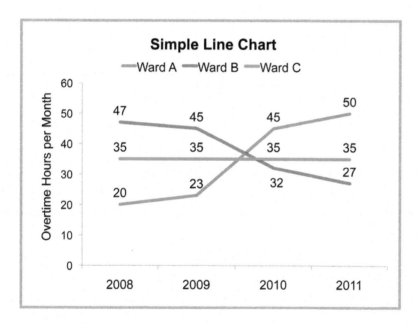

Fig. 6.7. Simple Line Chart

There are two other line chart variations that can be used to display these same data: a stacked line chart and a 100% stacked line chart. These are similar to stacked column and stacked bar charts in that the values at each time interval are added to the cumulative sum of previous series at that same time interval.

Figure 6.8 is an example of a stacked line chart using exactly the same data as that of Fig. 6.7.

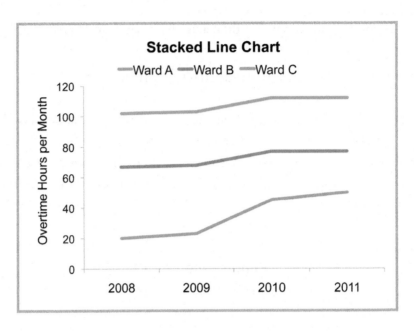

Fig. 6.8. Stacked Line Chart

Quite a different picture, isn't it? It now appears that all three wards show an increasing trend. Why does the stacked line chart in Fig. 6.8 show such a different picture than the simple line chart in Fig. 6.7?

If you examine Fig. 6.8, you'll notice that Ward A (the one with the upward trend in Fig. 6.7) is the first line on the bottom of the stacked chart. Since the values of the other two wards are added to these values, the values for Ward A literally push up the cumulative values for all other wards. This gives all lines an upward appearance, even Ward B, which has a pronounced downward trend in Fig. 6.7.

Figure 6.9 presents exactly the same data in another line chart variation, the 100% stacked line chart format.

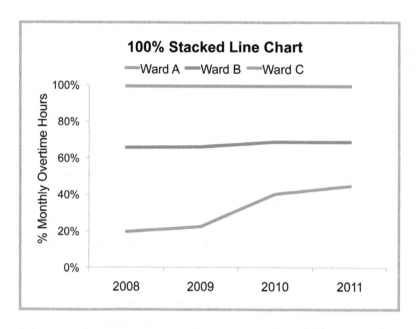

Fig. 6.9. 100% Stacked Line Chart

As with a stacked line chart, this 100% stacked line chart is very difficult chart to interpret when compared to the simple line chart, especially since the line for the series that appears at the top must, of necessity, be a flat line (representing a cumulative 100% value for each category).

As these examples clearly illustrate, it is very challenging to get information from a stacked or 100% stacked line chart because they require you to focus on the magnitude of the differences between lines at each successive x-axis interval. For this reason you should avoid using stacked and 100% stacked line charts unless there is some specific and unique type of data or situation for which they are particularly suited and the audience is accustomed to their use.

Run Charts

Line charts are often used in ongoing quality monitoring or in evaluating the effects of quality improvement initiatives. As highlighted

TIP

Ironically, if you perceive common cause variation erroneously as special cause variation and implement interventions in an attempt to reduce this variation (which is produced solely by the natural variability of the process), you will actually *increase* the variability of the process rather than decrease it.

IN PRACTICE

Run charts are very useful for evaluating pilot programs (e.g., on a single ward or single clinic). Small trials, referred to as "little bets" by Sims (2011), have been found to be quite valuable for large and small companies, and even for individuals (like comedian Chris Rock), before they decide to commit resources to a larger implementation.

in his very informative book *Data Sanity*, Balestracci (2009) notes that one of the major problems in the use of line charts is the tendency to look at deviations as if they were *special causes* (i.e., caused by factors not usually part of the process and requiring explanation) rather than as *common causes* (i.e., a normal part of the variability of the process itself). According to Balestracci,

> It's time to stop the plague of "management by little circles"—wasting time in useless meetings pouring over tables and tables of data, drawing little circles, and demanding explanations for why a number is different from either its predecessor or an arbitrary goal. (Balestracci, 2009, p. xi)

Carey and Lloyd (1995) make a similar point: "The first thing that happens when people do not understand variation is that they **see trends where there are no trends**" (p. 50, boldface in original).

One of the ways to avoid misinterpreting the importance of changes over time is to use a run chart, which is nothing more than a line chart with a reference line (typically the median) and a set of rules for determining whether a statistically significant change in the process has occurred. Run charts may be used to examine historical data over time or to evaluate the effect of a specific intervention implemented at a specific point in time. Balestracci (2009) refers to the run chart as "the most important initial analysis of a set of data" (p. 19).

Creating a Run Chart

The steps in creating a run chart are simple.

1. Create a line chart over time (days, weeks, months, successive patients).

2. Determine the median for these data, and draw a line across the chart at this median value. If you are examining

historical data over time, the median is computed for the entire dataset.

If you are assessing the effect of an intervention at a specific point in time, the median is computed for the pre-intervention period, and that value is projected for the post-intervention period. Enter new data points as new data become available.

3. Apply the rules for shift, trend, and total number of runs as indicated below.

The Institute for Healthcare Improvement (IHI, 2011) has published a run chart template on the web that calculates the median and creates a run chart. All you have to do is enter your data. The site also includes interpretive guidelines.

> **HOW-TO.** If you are setting up your own run chart template and accompanying chart in Excel in which you intend to add data as it becomes available, be sure to click on Select Data in the Design tab for the chart | Hidden and Empty Cells | Show Empty Cells as Gaps. This will prevent empty cells (i.e., those cells for which data will be entered as they become available) showing as zero values in your chart.

Interpreting a Run Chart

There are three rules for interpreting run charts in order to identify changes (Balestracci, 2009; Carey & Lloyd, 1995; IHI, 2011; Perla, Provost, & Murray, 2011).

Shift. A change in shift occurs if a designated number of *consecutive* data points are above or below the median. Values that fall at the median are ignored, and the count continues. If a single point falls on the other side of the median, the count must start anew. The IHI website and Perla et al. (2011) suggest a criterion of six or more consecutive points above or below the median. Carey and Lloyd (1995) suggest that with 20 or fewer "useful" data points (i.e., not on the median) seven data points should be required, and for 20 or more points eight data points should be required. Balestracci (2009) suggests a minimum of eight data points above or below the median.

The six or more rule can be used when you are initiating an intervention with a predicted direction of change and when you are counting data points following that intervention. The more rigorous criteria are appropriate when you are examining a historical process over a long period of time with no anticipation of change in a specific direction (Davis Balestracci, personal communication).

Trend. A change in trend occurs if a specified number of consecutive points continue up or down. If a single point reverses direction, the count must start anew. Points in the trend that are the same value as the previous point are ignored. The IHI website and Perla et al. (2011) suggest five or more consecutive data points. Carey and Lloyd (1995) suggest a criterion of 6 or more points for a chart with 9 to 20 points and a criterion of 7 or more for a chart with 21 to 100 points. Points on the median should be counted. Balestracci (2009) suggests a criterion of 6 or more consecutive points (5 if <20 data points).

The five or more rule can be used if you have implemented an intervention with a hypothesized direction of change and an evaluation of the points following that intervention. The more rigorous criterion (6 or more) should be used if you are analyzing a long historical sequence of data (Davis Balestracci, personal communication).

Total Number of Runs. A "run" is defined as one or more consecutive points above or below the median. Points landing exactly on the median are ignored. If the points are randomly distributed around the median, you would expect occasional runs both above and below the median and the number of these runs to be within a certain range depending on the total number of data points (subtracting those that fall precisely on the median). Tables of the expected number of runs for a given number of points are readily available (Balestracci, 2009; IHI, 2011; Carey & Lloyd, 1995). If the number of runs is either higher or lower than this expected range, it suggests that the process is not a random one—even if the decision rules for shift and trend have not been met. For example, with a sample of 20 points, the expected number of runs is between 6 and 15. If you have fewer than 6 or more than 15 runs in your data, the process is not likely a random one but rather one that involves a special cause.

Balestracci notes that,

Generally, a successful intervention will tend to create a *smaller than the expected* number of runs . . . . It is relatively rare to obtain more than the expected number of runs. In my experience, getting more runs than what one would expect randomly is due mostly to a data sampling issue. (Balestracci, 2009, pp. 149–150, italics in original)

Because of their simplicity of construction and ease of interpretation run charts are ideal for programs to track their own progress. Program staff can construct a simple run chart, enter their data as it becomes available, and interpret the results without complex statistics or outside help. Program staff retain ownership of the process and are no longer dependent on someone in Quality Improvement or another department to generate their performance charts.

How long it takes to identify a shift or trend using a run chart depends on the frequency of measurement. If data are collected daily (e.g., daily average wait time for clinic patients), a shift could be identified in as little as six days after an intervention and a trend in as few as five days. If, on the other hand, data are collected monthly (e.g., percent of missed appointments per month), it would take six months at the earliest to identify a shift and five months at the earliest to identify a trend. It is important to keep in mind, however, that often data that may typically be aggregated on a monthly basis (e.g., percentage of missed appointments) have a high enough frequency of occurrence to justify aggregation on a weekly or perhaps even a

IN PRACTICE

At one facility I asked different department heads, "Who creates your charts?" The answer was *always* the same: Jack in the Quality Improvement Department does them. If Jack left, became ill, or—God forbid—was hit by a truck, the facility's entire charting operation would come to a grinding halt. The use of simple run charts, completed at the program level, helps to decentralize some of this responsibility.

daily basis to enable more rapid evaluation of a specific intervention.

Let's apply the run chart methodology to the data on door-to-needle time presented in Fig. 6.1. Figure 6.10 presents these data with the pre-intervention median added.

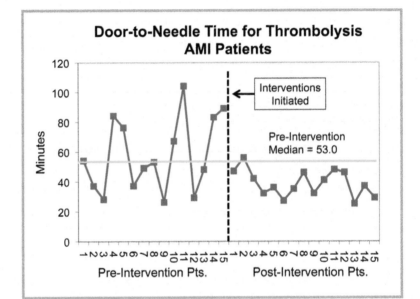

Fig. 6.10. Run Chart of Door-to-Needle Times for 30 Successively Admitted AMI Patients

TIP

Markers were added to the lines in Fig. 6.10 to facilitate counting. In this instance, it may not have been necessary since the lines show noticeable fluctuation from one point to the next but in instances where several values in a row are similar and the x-axis categories are close together, markers would be helpful.

When the door-to-needle times for six consecutive patients after the intervention were below the median for the baseline period (post-intervention Patients 3–9), this was an indication that the interventions introduced a statistically significant change in the process. The post-intervention period also appears to be associated with reduced variability. These are two critical aims of process improvement: improvement in the overall level of functioning and a reduction in the variability of the process.

There are additional techniques that can be used to identify special causes in a line chart over time (most notably, control charts), but they are beyond the scope of this discussion. Several sources provide information on the use and calculation of control charts with a focus on data from health care settings (Balestracci, 2009; Carey & Lloyd, 1995; Kelley, 1999).

Note that run charts (as well as control charts) can indicate whether your process has been affected by special causes, either positive or negative. If no special causes are identified, only common causes are present. These may result in a process that is unsatisfactory because either the average level of performance or its high degree of variability does not meet your expectations. In this case, the overall process should be examined further to identify any elements of the process which could be redesigned to improve performance. For example, if missed appointments are stable but at a level that is unsatisfactorily high, data on the process should be obtained to determine whether any elements of the appointment process could be modified to reduce the number of missed appointments.

Data Exploration

An important first step in exploratory data analysis is to examine your data unencumbered by hypotheses or summary statistical measures. Balestracci (2009) refers to this as "plotting the dots." Yau (2011) advises that you should "learn all you can about the data, and the visual storytelling will come natural" (p. 328). Cairo (2013), in relation to the creation of infographics, notes, "Sometimes it is not the story which leads you to search for a particular kind of data. Sometimes it is data that leads you to a story" (p. 160).

Here's a simple but compelling example of letting the data tell their own story. It was first brought to my attention by its description in Wainer (1997). It's a story of World War II and a man named Abraham Wald.

Abraham Wald was a brilliant mathematician who immigrated to the United States when the Nazis invaded Austria; he took a position at Columbia University in New York City. During World War II, the British were concerned about the losses of their bombers to enemy fire and wanted to put additional armor on the most vulnerable parts of the aircraft. To determine these vulnerable areas, they collected data on the damage due to enemy fire by meticulously measuring the precise location of each of the bullet holes in their bombers when they returned from a mission. The UK Air Ministry provided Wald with these data and asked if he could conduct a mathematical vulnerability analysis that would indicate where they should place additional armor.

One of the things that Wald did was to indicate the location of the bullet holes on a schematic outline of a bomber. After a period of time doing this, the schematic outline of a bomber marked with the location of bullet holes looked like the outline on the left in Fig. 6.11. After a longer time, it looked like the outline on the right.

Fig. 6.11. Pattern of Bullet Holes in British Bombers

Where should they put the extra armor? Think about it.

Many might be inclined to place the extra armor on those areas that had sustained the most damage. However, Wald suggested that they put the extra armor in the areas where there was no damage. Why? Because if a bomber was hit in either of these two areas, it never made it back to the airfield to have its bullet holes measured—it was downed by enemy fire. Wald didn't have to wrench the solution from the data, he just let the data speak, and they pointed to the solution.

Here's an example in the area of health care. In 1854 Dr. John Snow let the data speak to trace the source of a cholera epidemic in central London. On a street map, he indicated the location of all cholera deaths and all 11 water pumps. From the pattern of deaths and water pumps, he identified the Broad Street pump as the likely source of the contamination. He had the pump handle removed and that ended the epidemic. Snow's map and a brief description are presented in Tufte (1983).

As the examples of Wald and Snow clearly show, data are the key to problem solving. Levitt and Dubner, in their book *Freakonomics*, write:

> *Knowing what to measure and how to measure it makes a complicated world much less so.* If you learn how to look at data in the right way, you can explain riddles that otherwise might have seemed impossible. Because there is nothing like the sheer power of numbers to scrub away layers of confusion and contradiction. (Levitt & Dubner, 2005, p. 14, italics in original)

Read the last sentence of this quote again. In many problem-solving efforts, especially where everyone is busy blaming everyone else, obtaining clear and unbiased data will help point to a solution. Get the data and let the data speak. Data, collected properly, have no axe to grind; they just speak, sometimes quite elegantly.

In many cases problematic outcomes are the result of a method involving several process steps. This is as true of health care operations and patient care outcomes as it is of automobile manufacturing, retail operations, financial transactions, and the like. In this context, improving the outcome hinges on the identification of those few process steps whose improvement will result in the greatest improvement in the outcome. This involves identifying all the process steps, and the key to identifying *all* of these process steps is to involve line staff—those people who actually do the job—in this process. It has everything to do with the knowledge of how the

IN PRACTICE

One time a meeting of various staff (physicians, nurses, lawyers, others) was convened to develop a flowchart of the process to obtain legal permission to administer psychiatric medication over the patient's objection. It soon became apparent that the *only* person who truly understood this process was the secretary to the forensic psychiatrist. Had she not been there, the resulting flowchart would have been visually impressive but would have had gross omissions and inaccuracies.

current processes work and less on credentials, job title, and salary. As Berwick notes in a seminal article in the *New England Journal of Medicine*, "We must understand them [the complex production processes used in health care] before we can improve them" (Berwick, 1989, p. 55). Once these processes are identified, the next step is to collect data on them.

Two actual cases, using line charts over time as a starting point, illustrate the importance of data exploration.

Patient Escorts

One time after a presentation, a nurse asked me if I could help with a data problem she was having. The problem was that there were many complaints about the patient escort system (the system of volunteers who wheeled infirm patients to clinics and other needed services off their home wards). Complaints included the escorts being late or not arriving at all. She said that the facility director assigned her the responsibility of analyzing the problem and proposing a solution. She had collected very detailed data on escort usage for the past six months and had entered these data in a huge spreadsheet, but now she didn't know how to begin to analyze all these data. She had a three-week deadline to present her analyses and recommendations to the executive staff of the hospital. I agreed to help and asked her to email me the spreadsheet with the data.

There was a feeling in the hospital that the problems with the escort system were caused by the scheduling of too many appointments in the afternoon, resulting in an imbalance of escort demand and volunteer supply. Had this nurse decided to analyze the data for this specific effect (or worse yet, if she had only obtained tallies with a.m./p.m. and no specific times), she would have been asking the data to speak to her in *her* terms (a.m. vs. p.m.). In fact, had she done this, she would have found a relatively small increase after noon, which could not have accounted for the magnitude of the problems they were encountering.

IN PRACTICE

Frankly, given the size of the database and her relatively short time frame, I would have been much more anxious about the situation than she appeared to be. However, when I received her email with the attached spreadsheet, I knew she was quite anxious. She named the attached spreadsheet file "Lord_help_me_Smith.xls.

When I received the monstrous spreadsheet of data, the first thing I did was let the data speak in their own terms. Without fear of losing too much granularity, I aggregated the number of requests for escorts for each half-hour interval over the course of the day. Figure 6.12 presents the resulting chart based on the data from three long term care (LTC) units.

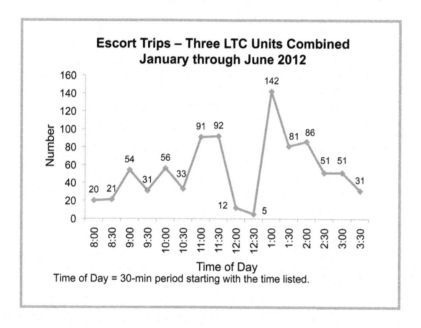

Fig. 6.12. Escort Trips by Time of Day in Half-Hour Intervals (Smith, 2013, reprinted with permission)

It's clear from this chart that there were gross imbalances in demand over the course of a day, a pattern that would have been obscured by a simple A.M./P.M. comparison. There were two peak periods, 11:00–12:00 and 1:00–2:30 (including an extreme outlier for 1:00–1:30). These peak demand periods resulted in the problems they were seeing. The imbalance could be addressed by increasing the supply of escorts at peak times of the day, or reducing demand at peak times by rescheduling clinics to underutilized times, or a combination of both.

The data had spoken. As Wainer (1997) observes, "A good graph is quiet and lets the data tell their story clearly and completely" (p. 11). It was very fortunate that the staff had collected data with the necessary granularity to enable the data to speak. Few uses the word "atomic" to refer to data collected in great detail and warns against collecting data at too high a level:

> By *atomic* I mean specified down to the lowest level of detail at which something might ever need to be examined . . . . It is essential for good decision making to have the ability to see all the way down to the specific details and to be able to *slice and dice* data at various levels as needed. One of the painful lessons learned in the early days of data warehousing was that if we leave out details below a particular level of generalization because we assume they will never be needed for analysis, we will live to regret it. (Few, 2009, p. 25, italics in original)

Missed Appointments

Though viewing longitudinal data at the most disaggregated level is an essential first step, sometimes a pattern is revealed only by subsequently aggregating it at a higher level. In one psychiatric inpatient facility, patients with significant non-psychiatric medical problems were seen by outside medical specialists (oncology, cardiology, gynecology, etc.) who would come to a consultants' building at the facility on specific days. These consultants, 18 in total, came on days and times of their own choosing. The problem for these consultants, and for the patients, was that patients would frequently miss their scheduled consultant appointments. To discover why this was happening, details on all missed appointments were obtained for a six-month period. The first step in analyzing these data—plotting the dots, in Balestracci's terms (2009)—was to present a chart of the total number of appointments on each of the sequential workdays over the six-month period. Figure 6.13 presents these data.

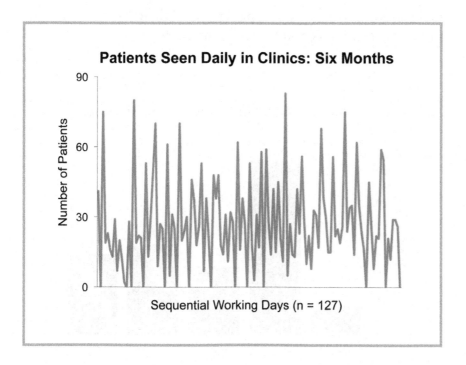

Fig. 6.13. Line Chart of Patients Seen in Clinics by Sequential Working Day

This chart reveals a very high degree of variability in the number of patients seen per day. In terms of process systems, this chart could appropriately be referred to as "chaos," with a range of 0 to more than 80.

In discussing this chart with line staff, it became apparent that many missed appointments occurred on high-volume days when the wards did not have enough escorts to take all the scheduled patients to their clinics in the consultants' building. Since some of these clinics were noncritical (e.g., routine follow-up appointments), nursing staff on the wards triaged which patients they would send to clinics and which would have to miss their appointments.

The key to solving this imbalance between supply and demand was to make the demand less variable, by reducing the number of appointments on high-volume days. A first step in this process was to determine if there were any patterns in high demand. Figure 6.14 shows the data aggregated by day of the week.

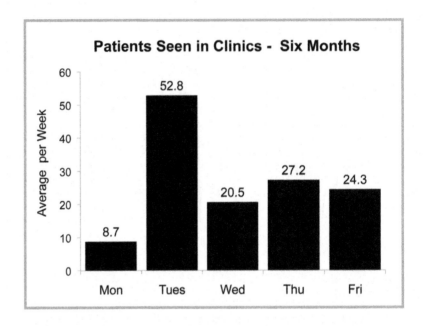

Fig. 6.14. Column Chart Highlighting Major Consultants on Tuesday

It's clear from Fig. 6.14 that there were gross imbalances in the average number of patients seen on specific days of the week, a pattern obscured by the daily data. The next step was to identify the medical specialists who were contributing to the high-volume of appointments on Tuesdays.

Figure 6.15 shows a stacked column version with the same data, in which the segments represent the volume of appointments on each day of the week, with the two highest volume consultants on Tuesday highlighted.

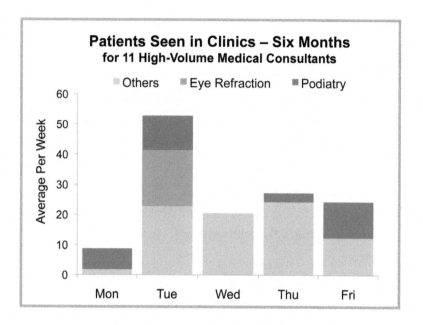

Fig. 6.15. Stacked Column Chart Highlighting Major Consultants on Tuesdays

These are just two small illustrations of process improvement using charts. In the improvement philosophy known as lean, the examples presented would be considered improvements in flow (Graban, 2012).

With the data presented in this way, the moves that have to be made to even out the demand are readily apparent—and those moves involve only 2 of the 18 consultants (only 11% of consultants). If you move Podiatry from Monday to Wednesday and Eye Refraction from Tuesday to Monday, you can level the demand—and the 16 other consultants never even knew there was a problem. *That's the power of letting the data speak.*

SUMMARY

- Line charts are very effective at displaying trends over time for either short or long periods of time.

- In contrast to column and bar charts, line charts can have a truncated y-axis.

SUMMARY *(continued)*

- To accurately portray trends for data collected at irregular time intervals, the x-axis time intervals must include time categories for which no data are available.

- Dual axis charts sometimes lead to faulty interpretations. A recommended alternative is to plot percent changes from a baseline for each of the two series.

- Run charts provide a simple and effective method of determining whether observed changes are real changes in a process (i.e., due to special causes) or merely part of the natural variation of the process (i.e., due to common causes).

- In exploring data, begin at the least aggregated level to let the data speak in their own terms. Aggregation may be useful subsequent to this.

- Of the seven variations of line charts available in Excel and listed in Appendix A, only two are useful (line and line with markers). Stacked lines and 100% stacked lines (with or without markers) should be avoided. A 3-D Line chart is so confusing it doesn't even deserve mention.

7

Displaying Proportions: Pie Charts

■ The use of pie charts and problems associated with their use

■ Alternatives to pie charts to show a part-to-whole relationship

The primary purpose of a pie chart is to show the proportion of various components contributing to a whole. Zelazny (2001) notes that "because a circle gives such a clear impression of being a total, a pie chart is ideally suited for the one—and only—purpose it serves: showing the size of each part as a percentage of some whole, such as companies that make up an industry" (p. 28). Pie charts were originally developed by William Playfair in 1801 and have a tremendous following, judging from their frequent use in financial, trade, newspaper, and scientific publications, as well as conference presentations and poster sessions.

Pie charts may be constructed and labeled either with percentages or raw numbers (e.g., number of events, dollars, etc.). The resulting pie will look exactly the same whether you enter raw scores or percentages.

An Application

Your facility has undertaken an effort to reduce the number of falls. To identify the major causes of falls, data have been collected on the causes over the past six months. Figure 7.1 shows a pie chart depicting the results.

> **TIP**
>
> Sometimes a pie chart with a legend will not include a legend key for all segments *and there will be no alert that this has occurred.* Whether this happens is dependent on the length of legend labels, their font size, the size of the computer screen, and the size of the chart. You should always check to see that there is a legend key for each segment.

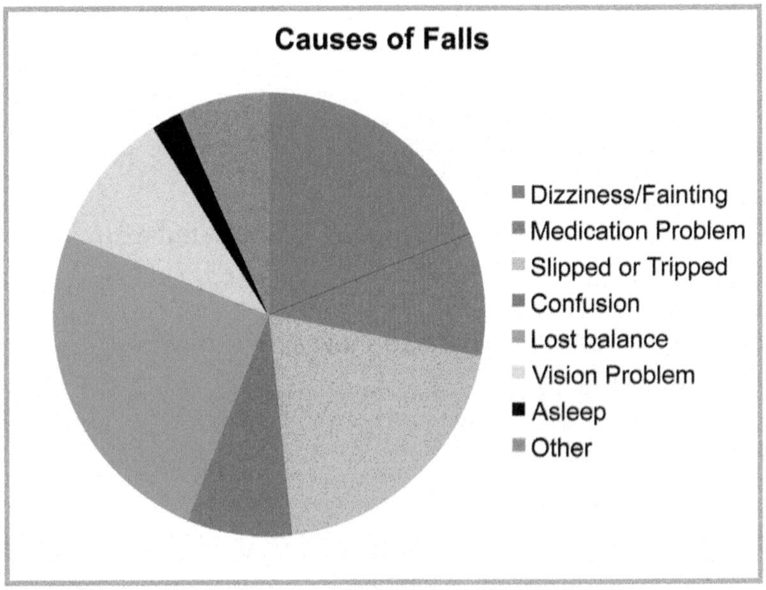

Fig. 7.1. Pie Chart of Causes of Falls

Figure 7.1 is colorful and gives a quick impression of the major differences in proportions of the causes of falls. However, it has two major shortcomings. First, the observer is unable to determine the exact size of the slices. For those who take their key from the angles at the center of the pie, Robbins (2005) notes that viewers underestimate acute angles (angles less than 90°) and overestimate obtuse angles (angles more than 90°). Kosslyn (2006) notes that the one fourth of viewers who focus on the relative areas will systematically underestimate the sizes of larger segments. Because of these problems, it is often difficult to rank slices based on their apparent size, especially when the sizes of the slices are similar.

The second problem with pie charts, as they are typically constructed, is that they require mental gymnastics to associate the color codes of the slices with the color codes in the legend. Sometimes, when there are many slices, the colors are hard to distinguish and to match with the small color keys in the legend. If you were asked to name the two highest causes of falls in Fig. 7.1, first you would have to make an educated guess as to the two largest slices and then you would have to match the color of the slices with the color code in the legend.

Those who like pie charts will readily point out that these two problems (uncertainty about values and matching slice color codes with legend color codes) can easily be remedied by redesigning the chart so that the data values and their associated category labels appear next to their respective slices (Fig. 7.2).

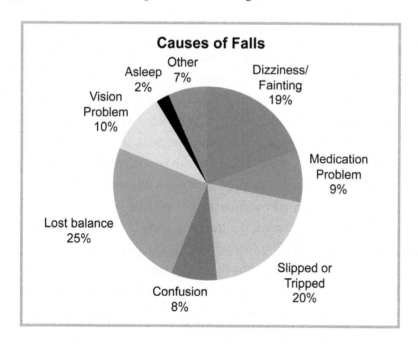

Fig. 7.2. Pie Chart With Category Name and Value Placed Next to Slice

Fair enough. It is now easy to see the legend for each slice and its associated percentage. Examine Fig. 7.2 and determine the two highest cause of falls. I'm sure you came up with the correct answers in relatively short order: Lost Balance at 25% and Slipped or Tripped at 20%.

If I were to ask how you determined the correct answer, most likely your response would be that you scanned the values and their associated labels around the periphery of the pie—with the actual pie shape playing a minor role, if any. (Isn't that how you did it?) As a matter of fact, finding the answer would probably take almost as much time with or without the actual pie.

By placing the legends and values next to the slices, you have made the pie chart more useful, and in so doing, you have made the pie graphic itself less useful. You have, as Few (2007) writes, "turned the pie chart into an awkwardly arranged equivalent of a table of labels and values" (p. 4). In essence, you have created a circular table.

HOW-TO. To insert labels in a pie chart, select the chart | Layout | Data Labels | and select the position where you would like the label to appear (e.g., Outside End). Once the labels are inserted, double left click on one of the labels. This will present you with a number of content options for the labels: Series Name, Category Name, Value, Percentage, and Show Leader lines. You can select as many as you want. Category Name and Value or Percentage are the usual choices. Once you have done this, delete the legend since the category names now appear outside each slice.

If you want to rotate the pie for a better fit for some labels, double left click on any segment of the pie and the Format Data Series menu will appear. The first series option will be a slide bar to change the angle of the first slice, from no rotation to full rotation, moving in a clockwise direction. Move this slide bar and release it to see the effect on the pie.

How could these data be presented in a pie chart in a way that the graphic itself would actually facilitate the answer to the question? One helpful approach would be to arrange the pie chart slices in a Pareto format from highest to lowest (Gabrielle, 2013; Jelen, 2011; Wong, 2010), ordering segments starting with the largest at the 12 o'clock position and continuing in a clockwise direction (Fig. 7.3).

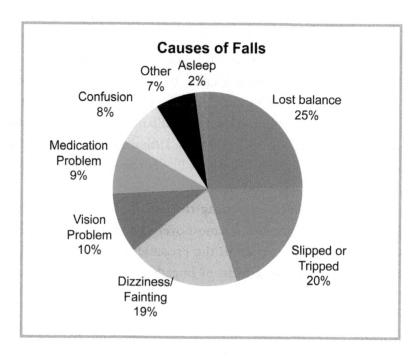

Fig. 7.3. Pie Chart in Pareto Format

You may have intentionally assigned specific colors to specific categories in your pie chart (e.g., green to Lost Balance in Fig. 7.2). However, colors are not assigned to categories in Excel but rather to sequential slices from the 12 o'clock position, counting clockwise. As you can see, when the data in Fig. 7.2 were sorted from high to low to create Fig. 7.3, green remains the color of the fifth slice which is no longer Lost Balance.

Pie Chart Armageddon

The battle lines have been drawn among chart designers when it comes to pie charts, with many experts on chart design disparaging the use of pie charts altogether—a few rather vehemently, characterizing them as "dumb," "mumbling," "useless," and even "hateful." According to Tufte (1983), in what is undoubtedly the most often cited quote about pie charts,

A table is nearly always better than a dumb pie chart; the only worse design than a pie chart is several of them, for then the viewer is asked to compare quantities located in spatial disarray both within and between pies . . . . Given their low data-density and failure to order numbers along a visual dimension, pie charts should never be used. (p. 178)

Few (2007) writes that "of all the graphs that play major roles in the lexicon of quantitative communication . . . the pie chart is by far the least effective. Its colorful voice is often heard, but rarely understood. It mumbles when it talks" (p. 1) and he concludes with the admonition that you should "save the pies for dessert" (p. 14). While expressing his admiration for William Playfair for his pioneering efforts in the late 18th and early 19th centuries in the invention and use of graphs, Few notes that Playfair invented the pie chart "on one of his off days" (2009, p. 15).

Jones (2007), while supporting the use of pie charts, indicates that "the familiar pie chart is the most overused, misused, and sometimes downright useless trick in the presenter's repertoire" (p. 19). Wainer (1997) expresses a form of buyer's remorse in reference to pie charts:

I used to like pie charts, but that was a long time ago. Now I hate them. What brought about this change of heart? Reasons for hating pie charts are so numerous that almost no explanation is necessary. What is more surprising is why I liked them originally. (p. 87)

What do these critics of pie charts recommend in their place? The answer is a column or bar chart arranged in a Pareto format, as in Fig. 7.4.

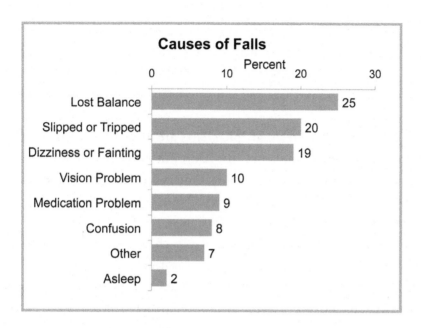

Fig. 7.4. Bar Chart in Pareto Format

This chart clearly and immediately shows the two highest causes of falls. It also highlights other facts about the data not as immediately apparent in the pie chart (like the gap between the third and fourth highest causes). Of a bar chart in Pareto format, Wainer writes, "I have yet to find a pie chart that cannot be improved in this way" (1997, p. 89).

Although many disparage the use of pie charts, they are not without supporters. Zelazny (2001) upholds the use of pie charts, though he notes that they are the least practical of the five major chart types (column, bar, line, pie, and scatter) and are the most misused and most abused. He cautions that pie charts should generally not be composed of more than six components. He also discourages their use when the objective is to make comparisons among two or more pies.

Kosslyn (2006) is of the opinion that pie charts can be used to convey an impression about proportions of a whole, but for precise estimations, pies should not be used. He supports the use of pies with explicit labels placed next to the segment and also the use of "exploded" slices, where one segment is removed slightly from the pie to highlight its importance. Wong (2010) also supports the use of pie charts for showing portions of a whole, but notes they shouldn't have more than five slices and cautions against using embellishments (like 3-D effects).

Jelen (2011) writes that "pie charts are great for comparing two to five different components" (p. 126), but notes that they are overused and many guidelines contraindicate their use. Rather than using multiple pies for comparisons, both Zelazny (2001) and Jelen (2011) suggest switching to 100% bars or 100% columns.

The most forceful supporter of pie charts is Gabrielle (2013), who feels that the blanket distain for them is overdone. While acknowledging that other types of charts may allow more precise comparisons, he points out that in some instances only approximate values are needed rather than precise comparisons. He takes issue with Tufte's claim that the only thing worse than a pie chart is to compare several of them. Gabrielle (2013) readily admits that while it may difficult to compare several pie charts with many slices, it is not difficult to compare pies composed of two slices each. He also notes that in a pie chart, it is immediately evident that the slices contribute to a whole, a feature that is not as apparent when these data are presented in a column or bar chart format. Adding text data to a bar or column chart to make this clear (e.g., a text box or sum of scores indicating 100%) introduces complexity to the chart. Finally, he asserts that the human visual system likes rounded shapes, and pie charts communicate emotionally in a way that bar charts do not, conceding, however, that the latter may be more important in some settings than in others. Gabrielle (2013) concludes:

> Tufte is wrong to make an assertion about pie charts based on his own context (the analysis and presentation of complex data) and use broad strokes to apply that to domains where he has no expertise (presenting and selling ideas in the boardroom). Pie charts have earned their place in your business presentations. (p. 4)

The bottom line is that the immediate recognition of a pie as comprising a whole is a strong point in the use of pies. When a single pie consists of only two slices and the category labels and values are clearly indicated either within the slices or adjacent to them, a pie can communicate quite effectively. That's why I prefer the chart on the left in Fig. 7.5 to the one on the right.

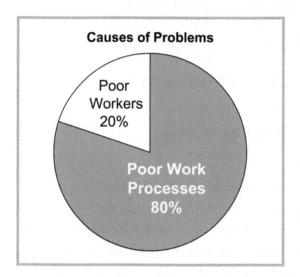 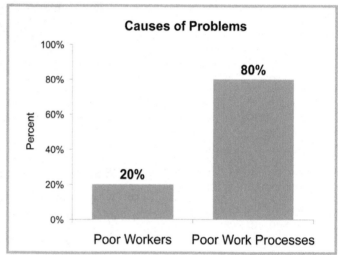

Fig. 7.5. Pie Chart and Column Chart of the Same Data

I also agree that comparisons among pies when there are only two slices can be effective and that they sometimes convey an emotional element that enhances the message. That's why I prefer Fig. 7.6 to a column chart with two columns of percent met.

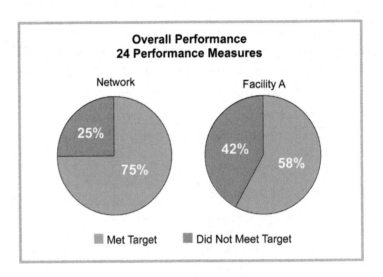

Fig. 7.6. Two Pies for Comparison Purposes

While pie charts may be useful in certain limited circumstances, the widespread criticism of them is justified in that *the predominant use of pie charts is to convey information on multiple categories, in no particular order, often with the labels in a legend box.* In this very common use, pie charts fail miserably to convey information quickly and easily to most observers.

Other Pie Chart Variations in Excel

What about the other pie chart variations available in Excel as listed in Appendix A?

An *Exploded Pie* involves separating *all* slices from each other and from the center by a space. This creates a rather odd-looking chart, and as Jelen (2011) points out, there is no need for this variation since it is simple to explode a single segment for emphasis.

Pie in 3-D introduces depth to the pie. As in other 3-D charts, the depth conveys no information and is unnecessary. While the default depth is minimal, often the y-axis and perspective values in the 3-D rotation are accentuated such that the pie pitches dramatically away from the viewer to emphasize the 3-D effect. This introduces a pronounced distortion, magnifying the size of the segments nearest the front. Of this type of chart, Jelen (2011) writes, "This is a cool effect when you are trying to decorate a PowerPoint chart. However, it is not as effective if you want someone to read and understand the data" (p. 126). That about says it all.

Pie of Pie involves one pie slice further segmented in another linked pie and *Bar of Pie* involves one pie slice further segmented in a single stacked bar. Try to think of another way.

Exploded Pie in 3-D (Fig. 7.7). Words fail . . . .

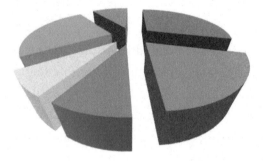

Fig. 7.7. Exploded Pie in 3-D

When it comes to using these other variations, it's clear that the farther your pie gets from being a simple pie with two slices, the farther your pie will be from being quickly and easily understood by most observers.

SUMMARY

- Pie charts can be useful in conveying information when only two segments are presented. When precise values are important, category names and data values (numbers or percentages) should be inserted either next to or within the slices to which they apply.

- With just two slices, pie charts can also be used to compare one time frame to another or one setting to another.

- Pie charts do a poor job conveying information on the proportions of many segments contributing to a whole.

- If a pie chart must be used to display the proportion of many segments adding up to a whole (e.g., your boss demands it), its information value will be improved by ordering the segments in a Pareto fashion, starting at the 12 o'clock position and moving clockwise.

8

Displaying Relationships: Scatter Charts

CHAPTER TOPICS

■ When to use a scatter chart

■ How to insert a trend line in a scatter chart

■ How to calculate the correlation between two sets of data

■ Cautions regarding the interpretation of correlations: statistical significance, nonlinearity, and causality

■ The use of scatter charts to assess the comparability of measures

■ What is unique about scatter charts with lines

The primary purpose of a scatter chart is to present a picture of the relationship between two sets of data. In charts covered previously, one axis consisted of either discrete categories or time/ sequence intervals, and the other axis was comprised of values. In scatter charts, both the x-axis and the y-axis are comprised of values.

The values can be on different measures (e.g., patient satisfaction and facility staffing ratios) or on the same measure (e.g., blood chemistry values obtained on identical samples on two different laboratory machines). Scatter charts, also known as scatter plots, are typically square (i.e., have a 1:1 horizontal to vertical aspect ratio).

Both axes of a scatter plot may be truncated, with each axis extending from just below the lowest obtained value on that axis to just above the highest obtained value. In creating scatter charts, it is customary to arrange the axes such that the lowest value of y-axis is at the bottom of the y-axis and the lowest value of the x-axis is on the left side of the x-axis.

When arranged in this way, scatter charts that show a consistent pattern of plotted points that move from the lower left to the upper right denote a positive relationship between the two variables (i.e., low values on one variable paired with low values on the other variable, high with high). Conversely, a consistent pattern of plotted points in a scatter chart that moves from the upper left to the lower right denotes a negative relationship (low values on one variable paired with high values on the other variable, high with low). The latter is also referred to as an inverse relationship. A random pattern of plotted points, with no clear up or down trend, suggests that there is little, if any, relationship between the two variables.

An Application

Suppose you were interested in the relationship between staff morale and the percent of missed appointments in primary care clinics. Table 8.1 presents hypothetical data on these two variables. Lower scores on the morale score indicate lower morale.

Table 8.1. Staff Morale Scores and Percent Missed Appointments for 10 PCS Clinics

Primary Care Clinic	Percent of Missed Appts. per Week	Staff Morale Score
A	1.3	33.1
B	14.8	22.8
C	2.9	28.8
D	4.9	28.7
E	10.1	24.5
F	7.5	29.4
G	8.4	26.6
H	9.6	27.5
I	12.4	26.5
J	4.2	32.5

Figure 8.1 presents a scatter chart of the data in Table 8.1 along with a linear trend line.

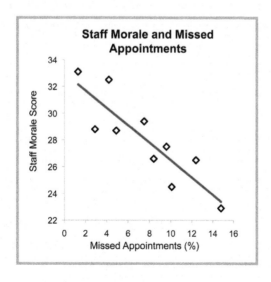

Fig. 8.1. Scatter Plot of Staff Morale and Missed Appointments

An examination of Figure 8.1 reveals that low percentages of missed appointments are associated with higher levels of staff morale and, conversely, high percentages of missed appointments are associated with lower levels of staff morale. More on this later . . . .

Trend Lines

Inserting a trend line in a scatter chart is easy in Excel (some might say too easy). The most frequently used trend line is a linear one, technically known as the least squares regression line. If the term "least squares regression line" brings up fearful images of your experience in STAT 101, fear not. This and a few other statistical concepts related to scatter charts (slope, intercept, and R-squared value) are explained in Appendix H.

TIP

Use caution in projecting trend lines. Do not project trend lines forward unless there is a clear trend in that direction. Sometimes an outlier or two can pull a trend line in a direction not characteristic of the majority of points in the scatter plot.

HOW-TO. Once you have created the scatter chart, click on the chart | Layout | Trendline | Linear Trendline. A line, the least squares regression line, will be inserted into your chart as in Fig. 8.1. You can also fit other curves to your data, project the trend line forward, insert the equation for this trend line, or insert an R-squared value—Layout | Trendline | More Trendline Options. See Appendix H for more information on these options.

Correlation Coefficient

A single number—technically known as the Pearson product-moment correlation coefficient—can be calculated to quantify the linear relationship between two sets of paired values. The correlation coefficient has a range from +1.00 (representing a perfect positive correlation: high associated with high and low associated with low) to –1.00 (representing a perfect negative correlation: high associated with low and low associated with high).

For the data in Fig. 8.1, the correlation coefficient between staff morale score and percent missed appointments is –0.87, a high negative correlation.

HOW-TO: The correlation coefficient between two sets of values can be easily computed in Excel or in the embedded Excel data-sheet in PowerPoint by following these simple steps.

1. Enter the data as displayed in Table 8.1 into a spread-sheet (or, if you've created this chart in PowerPoint, open the data sheet by right clicking on the chart | Edit Data).

2. Select an empty cell on the spreadsheet, not directly adjacent to the data array, and enter "=correl(" [without the quotation marks].

3. Hold the left mouse button down and run the mouse down the column Percent of Missed Appts. per Week. These cells will now be enclosed with a dotted line.

4. Release the mouse button and type in a comma.

5. Now hold the left mouse button down and run the mouse down the column of Staff Morale scores. These cells will now be enclosed with a dotted line.

6. Release the mouse button and type in a close parenthesis.

7. Hit Return and the correlation will appear. As indicated, in the example above, the value is –0.87.

IN PRACTICE

Sometimes data on one or the other or both sets of values are missing for a case or several cases. Excel auto-matically eliminates these cases from the calculations.

TIP

The calculation of correla-tions and many other statis-tical tests and functions can be found in the Formulas and Data | Data Analysis tabs on an Excel spread-sheet. For more information on these, consult books or websites on statistical func-tions in Excel.

Statistical Significance

In an experimental paradigm (e.g., testing an intervention), calculat-ing the statistical significance of the result gives you the probability that the result was due to chance (i.e., the normal variability of the process). If the probability of chance accounting for the results is

TIP

Sometimes correlations are computed between all possible pairs of a large array of variables. Given the large number of computed correlations, it is very probable that some will appear noteworthy and statistically significant merely due to chance factors alone. Focusing on these few can lead to invalid conclusions.

sufficiently low (typically $p < 0.05$), and you have designed your study well—to exclude factors other than your intervention—then you can conclude that your intervention was the cause of the result. However, statistical significance is not the same as practical importance. A statistically significant effect may have little practical importance (because the size of the effect is too small, or the intervention is not cost-effective, or any number of other factors).

The same is true of the statistical significance of correlations—a small but statistically significant correlation indicates that the relationship most likely did not occur by chance, but the relationship may have little practical importance. Tables and calculators to determine the statistical significance of correlations can be readily found online (e.g., Soper, 2013). They reveal that very small correlations can be statistically significant if the sample size is large enough. For example, a correlation of 0.09 obtained on a sample of 500 is statistically significant ($p < 0.05$). Yet, a correlation this low has very little value in a practical sense. That's why correlations are usually viewed in terms of their size rather than their statistical significance.

Table 8.2. Size of Correlations and Meaning (Smith, 2013, reprinted with permission)

Size of Correlations	
0.9–1.0	Very highly correlated
0.7–0.9	Highly correlated
0.5–0.7	Moderately correlated
0.3–0.5	Low correlation
< 0.3	Little if any correlation

Nonlinearity

If you find that the correlation between two variables of interest is very low (e.g., 0.09), why bother to plot it in a scatter chart? The answer is that you'd like to see the shape of the relationship. The Pearson product-moment correlation is a measure of *linear* correlation and is insensitive to relationships that are not linear. If there is a relationship, even a strong one, but it's not linear, the computed linear correlation will not detect this.

Figure 8.2 presents a scatter chart symbolically illustrating data collected by psychologists Robert Yerkes and John Dodson in 1908. As you can see, there is clearly a relationship between the two variables studied, but in contrast to the previous example, this relationship is curvilinear. As indicated, the calculated linear correlation is near zero ($r = 0.09$).

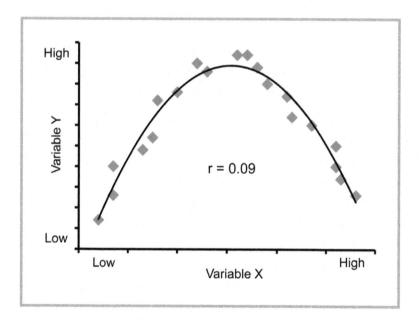

Fig. 8.2. Symbolic Illustrative Data from Yerkes and Dodson (1908).

Had Yerkes and Dodson computed a Pearson product-moment correlation between these two variables without plotting them and, finding no linear correlation, concluded no relationship existed, they would have missed discovering one of the fundamental laws of human performance. This law, appropriately named the Yerkes-Dodson Law, is that human performance (Variable Y) increases with increasing mental or physiological arousal levels (Variable X) *up to a point*. After that point, the arousal level becomes so high that it impedes performance.

The lesson from this illustration is that whenever you are interested in relationships between two variables, always plot them in a scatter chart to get a picture of the relationship. Scatter charts are one of the easiest ways to detect relationships of any kind (linear, curvilinear, J-shape, etc.).

Correlation and Causality

In Tufte's estimation, "the relational graphic—in its barest form, the scatterplot and its variants—is the greatest of all graphical designs. It links at least two variables, encouraging and even imploring the viewer to assess the possible causal relationship between the two plotted variables" (Tufte, 1983, p. 47). A key phrase in this quote is "to assess" since it is common knowledge that a high correlation (positive or negative) does not imply causality.

In examining Fig. 8.1, for example, it may seem intuitive that the high levels of missed appointments have a negative effect on staff morale. That may be true. But it may also be true that poor staff morale (i.e., a poor treatment milieu) and its impact on patients may be the cause of an increased number of missed appointments. Or it may be true that some other factor (a poor scheduling system, poor physical facilities, or poor leadership) may cause both poor staff morale and an increased number of missed appointments. In short, if two variables (*A* and *B*) are highly correlated, A may cause B, B may cause A, or a third variable C may cause both.

The question of cause and effect always arises when studies are designed to look at the relationship between variables as they exist in a sample or population (i.e., not in the context of a controlled trial involving random assignment to groups). Newspaper headlines reporting such studies often begin with "Study Links . . . ." Such was the case, for example, when early epidemiological studies linked postmenopausal estrogen therapy with decreased risk of coronary heart disease. Later controlled studies revealed that this relationship was most likely spurious, due to factors other than hormone replacement treatment (like the socioeconomic level of the group prescribed hormone replacement therapy and their diet and exercise habits).

Similarly, if you were to obtain data on a number of subjects and examine the relationship between exercise and cardiac disease, you most likely would find that there was a negative (inverse) relationship between the two: the higher the amount of exercise, the lower the risk of cardiac disease. But if you also obtained data on the number of exercise shorts owned by each of the subjects, you would also probably find an inverse relationship between the number of exercise shorts owned and cardiac risk (i.e., the more exercise shorts owned, the lower the cardiac risk). You wouldn't buy a case of exercise shorts to reduce your cardiac risk. Would you?

TIP

A classic example of the falsity of drawing conclusions based on correlational data is the fact that, over the course of a year, the number of ice cream cones sold in Times Square is highly correlated with the number of drownings at Coney Island. The key to this relationship is the temperature: warmer weather more of both, colder weather fewer of both. The next time you're tempted to draw conclusions based on correlational data, keep this example in mind.

Scatter Plots to Determine Comparability of Measures

Scatter plots are often used to determine whether measures obtained using two different methods are comparable (e.g., lab values on identical samples on two machines, subjective ratings on the same rating scale by two different raters).

An Application

You're a quality specialist in a laboratory, and recently your laboratory purchased a new analyzer. You want to compare the output of the new analyzer with that of the old analyzer to assess whether the new equipment gives values comparable to the old equipment.

You obtain measures of triglyceride levels from both machines on blood samples that have been split in half, one half analyzed by the old machine and one half by the new machine. Thus, for each sample you have two scores on identical samples: a triglyceride level obtained using the old machine and a triglyceride level obtained using the new machine (Table 8.3). (Of course, in an actual laboratory setting many more pairs of values would be utilized, and a number of additional statistical tests would be employed to determine the comparability of the two machines.)

Table 8.3. Hypothetical Triglyceride Levels Obtained on Two Machines

Sample	Old Machine	New Machine
1	96	100
2	120	125
3	57	60
4	130	130
5	110	102
6	139	142
7	85	85
8	149	140
9	116	115
10	110	107
11	64	66
12	71	78

Fig. 8.3 presents a scatter chart and accompanying trend line for these data.

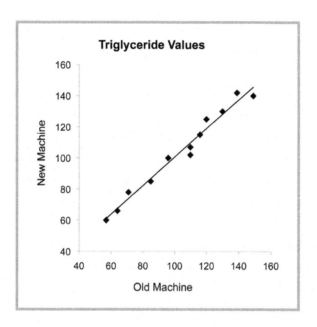

Fig. 8.3. Scatter Plot of Triglyceride Levels for Two Machines

As indicated in Fig. 8.3, low values on the old machine are associated with low values on the new machine. Similarly, high values on the old machine are associated with high values on the new machine. For the triglyceride example above, the correlation coefficient between values from the two machines is 0.99. Given this very high correlation between these two sets of data, you might be tempted to give the go ahead to replace the old machine with the new machine. Not so fast . . . .

Correlations and Means

Correlation coefficients tell you nothing, *absolutely nothing*, about the means of the two series of data. Even if the correlation were a perfect +1.00, the means could be vastly different.

IN PRACTICE

A t test of means in the case presented (i.e., with a value of 100 added to each of the values on the new machine) yields a t value of 70.6, p<.001), indicating a statistically significant difference between the two means.

TIP

Although you may have never thought of it in this way, the insensitivity of correlations to mean differences is the reason why correlations can be computed on two completely different measures with completely different scales.

If you need convincing, enter the data in Table 8.3 into a spreadsheet. At the bottom of each column of data, compute the mean; in another cell, compute the correlation using the method described above. The means are 103.9 for the old machine and 104.2 for the new machine—nearly identical. The correlation between the two is 0.99—nearly perfect.

Now change the values on your spreadsheet for the new machine by adding 100 to each of the new machine values. Thus, the first new machine value of 100 becomes 200, the second value of 125 becomes 225, and so on for all 12 values. What happened to the mean of the new machine? It increased by exactly 100 so it's now 204.2, nearly twice that for the old machine. Now check the correlation. It remained exactly the same—totally insensitive to the dramatic change in means. If these revised new machine values were the values actually obtained on the new machine (i.e., dramatically higher values than the old machine in all cases), would you still be comfortable replacing the old machine with the new machine on the basis of the high correlation between the two machines?

Why has the correlation not changed despite this dramatic difference in values? Because the correlation coefficient assesses the relationship between two sets of values in terms of high and low values. By adding a constant 100 to each and every value on for the new machine, you changed the values but never changed the high/low relationship among them. High values on the new machine remained paired with high values on the old machine, although they were now 100 points higher. Similarly, low values on the new machine remained paired with low values on the old machine.

Scatter Plot for More Than One Series

Scatter plots can be used to show the relationship between two variables for more than one series of data. Excel automatically assigns a different symbol and color to the data from the second series. Often it is advisable to make these symbols larger and more distinctive than the default settings (Fig. 8.4).

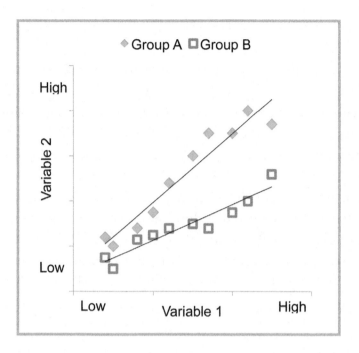

Fig. 8.4. Scatter Plot With Two Series

Where the groups are more concentrated in a cluster, different colored best-fit lines will help make clear which line goes with which data set. If there are many points in the plot that overlap each other, you can remove the fill color from the data points.

Scatter Chart With Lines

Excel offers four additional variations of scatter plots—smooth or straight lines connecting the plotted points, both with or without markers. Since scatter charts insert data points based on the values of each of the data pairs, it wouldn't seem to make any difference whether a pair like 47 (x-axis) and 68 (y-axis) was the first pair in your data array or the middle pair. It would still cause a data point to be placed in your scatter chart at the intersection of 47 and 68. Thus, the appearance of a standard scatter plot display of all your points would be the same regardless of the order in which pairs are entered into your array. However, this is not the case when using scatter charts with lines.

In scatter charts with lines (with or without markers), the lines are drawn sequentially from the first pair in the array to the next pair, and so on, throughout the array, thus introducing a third variable (represented by the data entry sequence) into the chart. Hence, the resulting scatter charts with lines will appear quite different dependent on the order of data entry.

The four charts in Fig. 8.5 display *exactly* the same data pairs, but with the data pairs entered in different orders. If you look closely at these charts, you will note that the data points in all four are exactly the same, but they are connected in a different sequence. The sample in the lower right has the data sorted by x-axis value from lowest to highest.

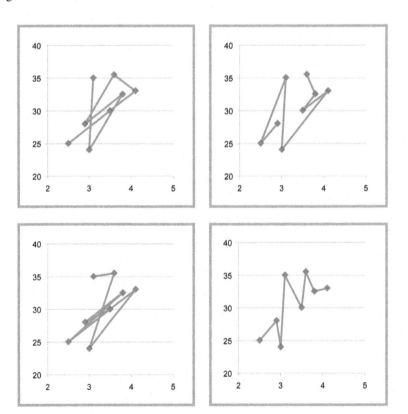

Fig. 8.5. Scatter Charts With Lines—Data Pairs the Same, Order of Data Entry Different

I have never seen scatter charts with lines used in a health care setting, but they have, on occasion, been used in other settings. Hannah Fairfield (2010) developed a scatter chart with lines to show the relationship between driving habits and gasoline prices for the period 1956–2010. In this chart, the x-axis is miles driven per capita, the y-axis is the price of a gallon of gasoline, and the data are entered sequentially by year from 1956 through 2010. Over this extended time period, the overall trend indicates an increasing number of miles driven (x-axis). However, in some years a number of factors, including increasing gasoline prices, combine to reduce the number of miles driven to a level below that of the previous year. When this happens, the line reverses direction and moves slightly from right to left.

TIP

Fairfield's scatter chart with lines may be found at http://www.nytimes.com/2010/05/02/business/02metrics.html?ref=hannahfairfield&_r=0

SUMMARY

- Scatter charts are used when both the y-axis and the x-axis are composed of values.

- Trend lines can help show the relationship between two sets of values and are easy to insert.

- A correlation coefficient quantifies the linear relationship between two variables, but the data should always be plotted to identify any possible nonlinear relationship.

- The most important aspect of a correlation coefficient is its size. Low correlations can be statistically significant if the sample size is large, but they are of little practical value.

- A correlation between two variables (*A* and *B*) does not imply causation. *A* may cause *B*, *B* may cause *A*, or they both may be caused by a third variable, *C*.

SUMMARY *(continued)*

- Correlation coefficients tell you nothing, absolutely nothing, about the comparability of the means of the two variables.

- The appearance of a scatter plot with lines is totally dependent on the order in which the data pairs are entered.

9

Area, Stock, Surface, And Doughnut Charts

Area Charts

Area charts are line charts with the area between each line and the x-axis filled in with a color. With a single series of data, whether you prefer a simple line chart or an area chart is a matter of taste. However, keep in mind that since area is the major focus of this display, as it is in column and bar charts, the y-axis should not be truncated.

The major problem with area charts occurs when there are two or more data series. In these instances, the fill for the series in the foreground may totally obscure some data points for the series in the background. Microsoft Corporation (2011) acknowledges this problem with Excel 2007 and suggests a remedy that also applies to Excel 2010.

> Unfortunately, data series with smaller values that are plotted in the back of an area chart may be completely or partially hidden behind data series with larger values that are plotted in front of them. However, in Microsoft Office Excel 2007, you can use transparency to show the entire outline of smaller data series through any larger data series in front. (p. 1)

While making the fill in the foreground somewhat transparent may sometimes help where there are just two series (dependent on the data), the problem with hidden data becomes really acute when the chart involves more than two series. Figure 9.1 presents an area chart with three series. It employs the transparency option suggested by Microsoft for the two series in the foreground.

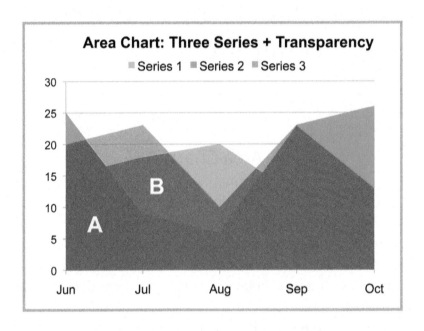

Fig. 9.1. Area Chart With Three Series (Two Semitransparent)

In addition to being almost impossible to follow the various series, this chart's transparency option now generates two rather prominent colors, brown (designated as *A* in Fig. 9.1) and purple (designated as *B*), neither of which is included in the legend.

Stacked and 100% stacked area charts present the same problems in obtaining information quickly and easily as do stacked line charts. Yau (2011), for example, notes that "one of the drawbacks to using stacked area charts is that they become hard to read and practically useless when you have a lot of categories and data points" (p. 166). Stacked and 100% stacked area charts should be avoided.

Stock Charts

Stock charts are typically used for plotting movements in the stock market. Excel has four variations including the familiar candlestick pattern, as shown in Fig. 9.2.

The high-low-close chart may be useful in some non-stock contexts where, for example, you may want to show means or medians and separately calculated ranges around them.

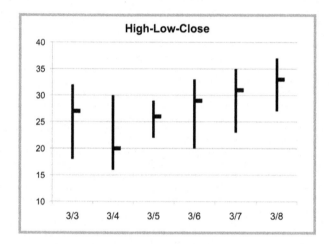
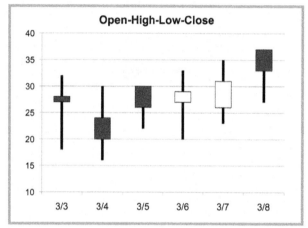
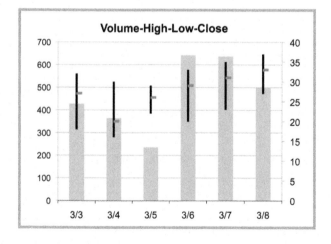
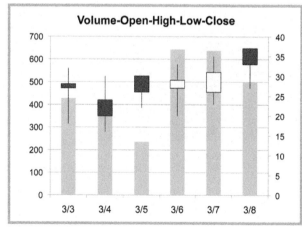

Fig. 9.2. Excel Stock Chart Variations

Surface Charts

Surface charts depict values for three variables: an x-axis variable, a y-axis variable, and a z-axis variable (depth). Excel has four variations of surface charts, as shown in Fig. 9.3. They look like topographic maps; colored segments represent the value ranges of the z-axis variable.

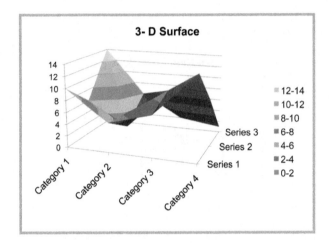

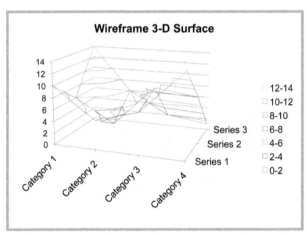

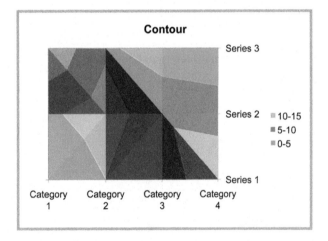

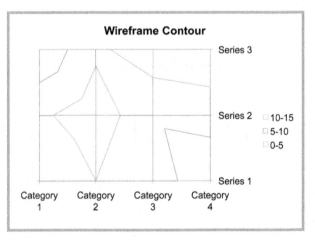

Fig. 9.3. Excel Surface Chart Variations

If you're confused by these, you're not alone. Jelen (2011) writes, "It is difficult to find a dataset that looks cool with a surface chart, and after you have found an appropriate dataset, it is often difficult to make out the valleys that might occur within the dataset" (p. 151).

I'm sure surface charts are useful to some in some specialized areas, but I've never used them myself nor have I seen them used in a healthcare setting.

Doughnut Charts

A doughnut (donut) chart is a pie chart with a hole cut in the middle. Excel has two variations of doughnut charts: a simple doughnut chart and an exploded doughnut chart. If you don't like pie charts, you're certainly not going to like doughnut charts, since they eliminate the angles in the center, the element upon which many base their judgment of slice size. Figure 9.4 presents examples doughnut charts involving one and two series of data.

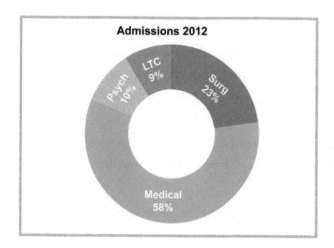 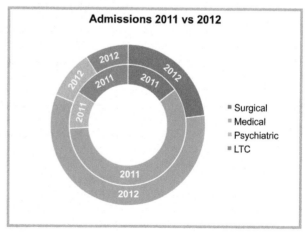

Fig. 9.4. Doughnut Charts With One and Two Series of Data

"Simply and easily" is not a phrase that comes to mind with doughnut charts, especially those involving more than one series. Nonetheless, some authors have little difficulty with multiple series doughnut charts (Jacobs, Frye, & Frye, 2007). Jelen (2011) refers to a doughnut chart as a "strange" chart but allows that it can sometimes be used to compare two pie charts. However, he admits that a 100 percent stacked column chart with one column for each series is usually better for this function. Others are not so kind.

Jones (2007) writes, "I'm not sure what use a donut chart might have for you, except perhaps to perplex your audience" (p. 38). Few (2012) writes that "if pie charts are graphical pastries filled with empty calories, donut charts are the same and more" (p. 271). The blog Junk Charts (2005) refers to a donut chart as "a useless chart made worse" (p. 1).

Did I mention previously that the battle lines were drawn on pie charts? Doughnut charts join pie charts as foot soldiers in this battle. I recommend not using doughnut charts.

SUMMARY

- Area charts may be used when there is but one series of data. Area charts for more than one series of data or stacked or 100% stacked area charts should generally be avoided.

- Stock charts are useful for portraying the movement of stocks. The High-Low-Close variation may be useful in other contexts.

- Surface charts seem to have little value in applied healthcare settings.

- Doughnut charts only accentuate the problems associated with pie charts. They should be avoided.

Bubble And Radar Charts

Bubble Charts

Bubble charts are similar to scatter charts but depict values on three dimensions: a value plotted on the x-axis, a value plotted on the y-axis, and a value communicated by the size of the bubble marking the data point.

An Application

Suppose you were interested in showing the relationship among performance score, patient satisfaction, and bed capacity for 10 hospitals, as presented in Table 10.1.

Table 10.1. Hypothetical Data for 10 Hospitals

Hospital	Performance Score	Percent Satisfied	Bed Capacity
A	80	80	738
B	92	92	172
C	85	93	247
D	97	97	109
E	75	85	394
F	89	98	62
G	90	87	123
H	85	80	350
I	96	90	73
J	83	87	147

A bubble chart of these data is presented in Fig. 10.1. Performance score is presented on the x-axis, satisfaction score on the y-axis, and bed capacity by the size of the bubble marker. Axis titles were added and a shape (●) added to the chart title to indicate that the bubble represents bed capacity.

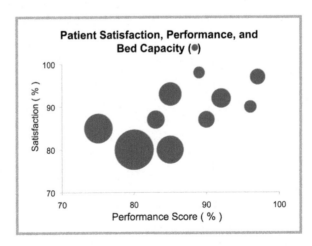

Fig. 10.1. Bubble Chart of Performance, Satisfaction, and Bed Capacity

The interpretation of Fig. 10.1 would be that higher performance scores and higher satisfaction scores tend to be associated with smaller sized facilities. However, the fact that bubble charts are correlational in nature and are best suited for small samples makes interpretations based on these charts very tentative.

The creator of a bubble chart has the option of the basing the relative size of the bubbles on area or diameter (Fig. 10.2). In both charts in Fig. 10.2, the larger bubble represents 800 beds, and the smaller bubble represents 200 beds, a 4:1 ratio.

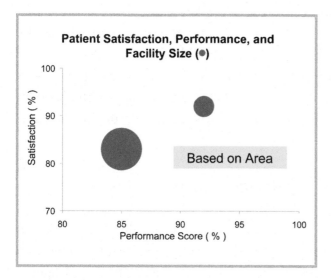 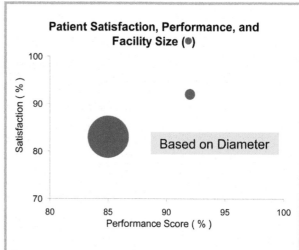

Fig. 10.2. Bubble Size Based on Area and Diameter

The default in Excel is to base the size of the bubbles on their areas. Comparisons on the basis of area are more accurate than those based on diameter (Jelen, 2011; Jones, 2007; Wong, 2010). Note how the chart based on area in Fig. 10.2 appears to visually approximate the true 4:1 ratio, while the chart based on diameter appears to show a much greater difference.

If some circles obscure part or all of smaller circles, you can leave the circles unfilled so that just the outline of the circle appears. As you might imagine, bubble charts, whether with filled circles or empty circles, can get quite visually complex as the number of data points increases.

The website www.gapminder.com has some truly remarkable displays utilizing animated bubble charts. One of these is called the Wealth & Health of Nations. In this chart, income per person is on the x-axis and life expectancy in years is on the y-axis. Each bubble represents a different country. The size of the bubble denotes the population of the country and the color of the bubble indicates the continent. There's an engaging video of this bubble chart, animated over two centuries, at http://www.youtube.com/watch?v=BPt8ElTQMIg (note: the letter between E and T is a lower case L).

In Excel there are only two variations of bubble charts (Appendix A). The second variation is the 3-D bubble chart. This 3-D variation is not as distorting as 3-D variations of other chart types since it merely replaces the circles with spheres. Though more complex than some of the basic charts, bubble charts may have value in some circumstances.

Radar Charts

Radar charts are rather strange looking at first sight. They have lines radiating out from the center (like bicycle spokes) and circular lines (like spider webs) around the inside of the circle. The bicycle spokes are akin to the x-axis categories of a column chart, and the spider web lines are akin to the y-axis values of a column chart. Because of the multiplicity of lines in a radar chart, the use of data labels is not advised.

An Application

A radar chart depicting the average rainfall in inches by month for two cities (New York and Seattle) is presented in Fig. 10.3. Data were obtained from weatherbase.com. The spokes from the center denote months with their labels depicted around the periphery. The average precipitation for each month is shown by its distance from the center point (the further the distance, the greater the average precipitation per month).

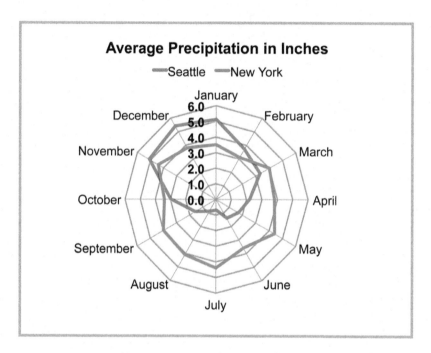

Fig. 10.3. Radar Chart of Average Precipitation in Inches for Seattle and New York City

As you can see, for the month of July, Seattle had an average precipitation of less than 1.0 inch, while New York City had an average precipitation of over 4.0 inches. You will also note that New York City had an average precipitation that was greater than that for Seattle for eight months of the year (March through October). Why, then, does Seattle have its rainy reputation?

The radar chart in Fig. 10.4 helps to explain Seattle's reputation. Instead of the average number of inches of precipitation per month, Fig. 10.4 depicts the average number of days per month *with any precipitation.*

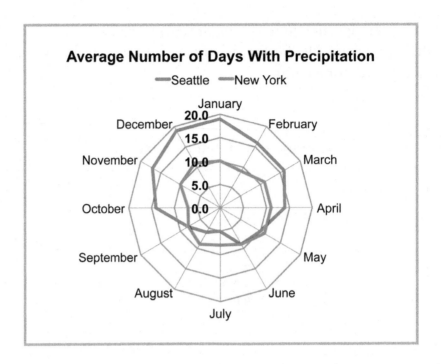

Fig. 10.4. Radar Chart of Average Days of Precipitation for Seattle and New York City

TIP

The interpretation of a radar chart is facilitated if there is a logical order to the arrangement of categories around the periphery (e.g. clock time, successive months).

In January, for example, Seattle had 19 days with precipitation, while New York City had only 10 days with precipitation. Seattle had more or an equal number of days with some precipitation than New York City for nine months of the year. The only exceptions were May, July, and August. That's why Seattle has the reputation it has. It has many more days of precipitation than New York but, overall, not as much precipitation in inches.

How might a radar chart be used in a health care or other applied setting? Jelen (2011) says that while radar charts are rarely used, they are great for performance reviews, showing how a person performed in a number of different areas. Other authors have also suggested that radar charts, because of their circular nature, are particularly useful for displaying data by clock hours (Jacobs et al., 2007). Thus, a radar chart could be used to display average emergency room (ER) wait time by time of ER presentation.

A radar chart can also be used to display performance on a number of measures, each with its own individual target. Suppose you had eight performance measures and you wanted to show your facility's performance on each of these measures against their individual targets. You could use a table, or you could use a bar chart with a bar for performance and a bar for target for each of the performance measures, as in Fig. 10.5.

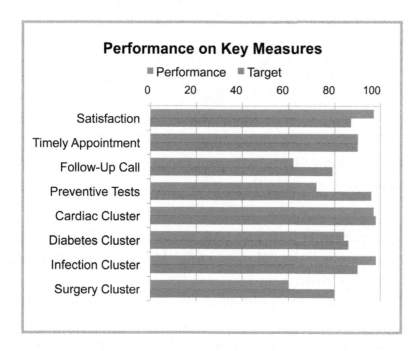

Fig. 10.5. Bar Chart: Performance and Targets for Eight Different Performance Measures

Or you could use a radar chart, as in Fig. 10.6.

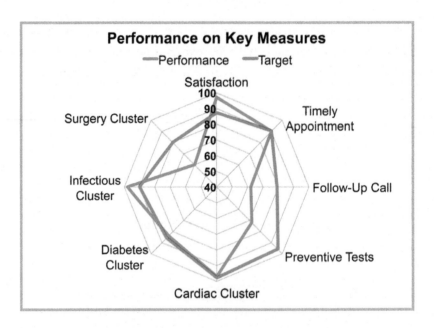

Fig. 10.6. Radar Chart: Performance and Targets for Eight
Different Performance Measures

Which chart, Fig. 10.5 or 10.6, shows how the facility is performing more quickly and more easily? My choice would be Fig. 10.6, the radar chart.

You can use a radar chart, as in Fig. 10.6, to provide a general overview of performance. However, because of their lack of precision, you would never track monthly changes in performance by presenting radar charts monthly or ask viewers to compare two or more radar charts.

There are two additional variations in Excel for radar charts as listed in Appendix A: Radar with Markers and Filled Radar. Both of these variations only increase the complexity of the chart and, if you use a filled radar chart, one series may obscure some or all of another series. They should be avoided.

SUMMARY

- Bubble charts may be useful in some situations to depict the relationship among three variables. Area, the default metric in Excel, should be used to create bubble size.

- Radar charts may be useful in some situations.

- Both bubble and radar charts are not useful when precise values are needed, for example, in tracking small changes over time. In these cases another type of chart or a table should be used.

- Keep in mind that many are not familiar with either bubble or radar charts. In deciding whether to use them, their unique information value should be balanced against the time and possible confusion induced in explaining how they are constructed and interpreted.

Final Thoughts

Creating informative Excel charts involves four aspects: knowing the story in your data, knowing the principles of chart selection and design, knowing how to implement these principles in Excel, and practice.

Knowing the Story in Your Data

Knowing the information you want to convey is critical to good chart creation. Sometimes you have a hypothesis, and the test of that hypothesis is the story. Sometimes you don't know what the story is until you have collected the data; such is the case when you are collecting process data to identify a process element for improvement.

In either case, after collecting the data, you may have to explore the data in several different ways to learn what they tell you. This could involve the aggregation or disaggregation of data, statistical analysis, the development of pilot charts, further discussion with those involved with the process or data collection, or other activities. Some of this may lead to the need for additional data. Once you're convinced that you have your hands around the data and know what the most critical information is, then you must think of how best to convey this information to your audience. Perhaps it will take the form of a chart or a series of charts, or perhaps some other format will be more suitable.

If your story will be elucidated in a series of charts, it is important to ensure not only that the information in each chart is conveyed clearly, but also that the overall story, conveyed in your sequence of charts, is clearly told. This is especially true when you are building a case for a certain action, whether it be introducing clinic telephone reminders facility-wide, changing a clinical guideline, or making the case for increased staffing. Weissman (2003) writes,

> I liken making presentations to massage therapy. The good massage therapist never takes his or her hands off your body. In the same way, the good presenter never lets go of the audience. The good presenter grabs their minds at the beginning of the presentation, navigates them through all the various parts, themes, and ideas, *never letting go*, and then deposits them at the call to action. (p. xxxviii, italics in original)

What a great image! How many presentations have you attended where you found yourself in the grip of the presenter? Where the logical flow was so clear and compelling that you *wanted* to see the next slide? Where you experienced yourself getting on a train of thought at the first stop and getting off at some considerable distance from there, after an exhilarating and enjoyable ride? If the results of David Paradi's survey (Paradi, 2013) are any indication, I daresay you've probably experienced very few of these occasions.

Knowing the Principles of Chart Selection/Design and How to Implement Them

Hopefully, after reading this book, you know the principles of good chart design and, if you create your own charts, how to implement these in Excel. It should be apparent that of the 73 chart types and variations available in Excel, only slightly more than a dozen are useful for the data typically found in a health care or other applied setting. Keeping the flowchart of the Big Five (provided in Chapter 2) handy will help to avoid some of the major chart selection mistakes associated with the most frequently used types of charts.

Practice

Developing a skill in any area requires practice. Yau (2011) summarizes this nicely with regard to visualization and information graphics when he writes,

> You don't have to be a great designer to make great graphics. You don't need a statistics PhD either. You just need to be eager to learn, and like almost everything in life, you have to practice to get better. (p. xxiv)

Practice with Excel software techniques is important if you create your own charts. With just a handful of charts, you will learn through repetition how the software works (changing chart types, formats, colors, etc.).

But you also need practice in applying the principles of good chart design to a wide variety of data. You can work on this aspect in the charts you create, but if your data are limited, your opportunities for practice will be similarly limited. Thankfully, there are many more frequent opportunities to hone your skills in applying the principles of good design. Just look more closely and carefully at the charts you see in your work setting, journals, conference presentations, poster sessions, newspapers, magazines, and the like. When you look at these charts, practice identifying chart design errors: poor selection of chart type, inappropriate value axis truncation, missing or misleading labeling, distracting elements, confusing color coding, and so forth.

Trust me. There are plenty of opportunities for practice in the world of charts out there.

Further Reading

I hope that I have stimulated your interest in chart design, and perhaps now you have a desire to know more about charts, either the basic ones covered here or other chart types. If so, I would recommend any of the books by Stephen Few. I have found them to be comprehensive, well-organized, thoughtful, and engaging.

If you want to read more about Excel software as it relates to charts, I would recommend the book by Jelen (2011). It contains all that you might ever want to know about the software behind creating charts in Excel.

There are also a host of websites, blogs, YouTube videos, and other materials on the Internet related to charts and chart design. Some of the authors of books on charts have their own websites and blogs. But be discriminating; there's a great deal of misleading information posted on charts.

Finally, thanks for reading this book. I hope that I have been helpful in enabling you to improve the charts you create.

References

Balestracci, D. (2009). *Data sanity: A quantum leap to unprecedented results*. Englewood, CO: Medical Group Management Association.

Berwick, D. M. (1989). Continuous improvement as an ideal in healthcare. *New England Journal of Medicine*, 320(1), 53–56.

Bonetti, P. O., Waeckerlin, A., Schuepfer, G., & Frutiger, A. (2000). Improving time-sensitive processes in the intensive care unit: the example of 'door-to-needle time' in acute myocardial infarction. *International Journal for Quality in Health Care*, 12(4), 311-317.

Cairo, A. (2013). *The functional art: An introduction to information graphics and visualization*. Berkeley, CA: New Riders.

Carey, R. G., & Lloyd, R. C. (1995). *Measuring quality improvement in healthcare: A guide to statistical process control applications*. New York, NY: Quality Resources.

Cleveland, W. S. (1985). *The elements of graphing data*. Monterey, CA: Wadworth Advanced Books and Software.

Fairfield, H. (2010, May 1). "Driving shifts into reverse." New York Times. Retrieved from http://www.nytimes.com/imagepages/2010/05/02/business/02metrics.html?ref=business

Few, S. (2004). Rare business assets: Tables and graphs that communicate. *Perceptual Edge*. Retrieved from http://www.perceptualedge.com/images/MessagetoExecutives.pdf

Few, S. (2007, August). Save the pies for dessert. *Visual Business Intelligence Newsletter*. Retrieved from http://www.perceptualedge.com/articles/08-21-07.pdf

Few, S. (2008, March). Dual-scaled axes in graphs: Are they ever the best solution? *Visual Business Intelligence Newsletter*.

Retrieved from http://www.perceptualedge.com/articles/visual_business_intelligence/dual-scaled_axes.pdf

Few, S. (2009). *Now you see it: Simple visualization techniques for quantitative analysis*. Oakland, CA: Analytics Press.

Few, S. (2012). *Show me the numbers* (2nd ed.). Burlingame, CA: Analytics Press.

Few, S. (2013). *Information dashboard design: Displaying data for at-a-glance monitoring* (2nd ed.). Burlingame, CA: Analytics Press.

Gabrielle, B. (2013, March 18). Why Tufte is flat-out wrong about pie charts. *Speaking PowerPoint*. Retrieved from http://speakingppt.com/2013/03/18/why-tufte-is-flat-out-wrong-about-pie-charts/

Gladwell, M. (2000). *The tipping point*. New York, NY: Little, Brown.

Graban, M. (2012). *Lean hospitals: Improving quality, patient safety, and employee engagement* (2nd ed.). Boca Raton, FL: CRC Press.

Handfield, R. (2004, February 1). Managing maverick spend at Deere and Delphi: An interview with Jon Stegner. Supply Chain Resource Consortium (SCRC). Retrieved from http://scm.ncsu.edu/scm-articles/article/managing-maverick-spend-at-deere-and-delphi-an-interview-with-jon-stegner

Harris, R. L. (1999). *Information graphics: A comprehensive illustrated reference*. New York, NY: Oxford University Press.

Heath, C., & Heath, D. (2010). *Switch: How to change things when change is hard*. New York, NY: Broadway Books.

Institute for Healthcare Improvement (IHI). (2011). Run chart tool. Retrieved from http://www.ihi.org/resources/Pages/Tools/RunChart.aspx

Jacobs, K., Frye, C., & Frye, D. (2007). *Excel 2007 charts made easy*. New York, NY: McGraw-Hill.

Jelen, B. (2011). *Charts and graphs: Microsoft Excel 2010*. Indianapolis, IN: Que.

Jha, A. K., Perlin, J. B., Kizer, K. W., & Dudley, R. A. (2003).

Effect of the transformation of the Veterans Affairs Health Care System on the quality of care. *New England Journal of Medicine*, 348(22), 2218–2227.

Jones, G. E. (2007). *How to lie with charts*. Santa Monica, CA: LaPuerta.

Junk Charts. (2005, July 22). Donuts and pies: Which tastes worse? [Blog post]. Retrieved from http://junkcharts.typepad.com/junk_charts/2005/07/pie_charts.html

Kelley, D. L. (1999). *How to use control charts for healthcare*. Milwaukee, WI: ASQ Quality Press.

Kosslyn, S. M. (2006). *Graph design for the eye and mind*. New York, NY: Oxford University Press.

Levitt, S. D., & Dubner, S. J. (2005). *Freakonomics*. New York, NY: William Morrow.

Malamed, C. (2009). *Visual language for designers: Principles for creating graphics that people understand*. Beverly, MA: Rockport.

Microsoft Corporation. (2011). Present your data in an area chart. Retrieved from http://office.microsoft.com/en-us/excel-help/present-your-data-in-an-area-chart-HA010218671.aspx

Paradi, D. (2013). Latest annoying PowerPoint survey results: Results of the 2013 Annoying PowerPoint survey. Retrieved from http://www.thinkoutsidetheslide.com/free-resources/latest-annoying-powerpoint-survey-results

Perla, R. J., Provost, L. P., & Murray, S. K. (2011). The run chart: A simple analytical tool for learning from variation in healthcare processes. *BMJ Quality and Safety*, 20, 46–51.

Perlin J. B., Kolodnor, R. M., & Roswell, R. H. (2004). The Veterans Health Administration: Quality, value, accountability, and information as transforming strategies for patient-centered care. *American Journal of Managed Care*, 10 (part 2), 828–836.

Robbins, N. B. (2005). *Creating more effective graphs*. Hoboken, NJ: Wiley.

Saber Tehrani, A. S., Lee, H. W., Mathews, S. C., Shore, A., Makary, M. A., Pronovost, P. J., & Newman-Toker, D. E. (2013). 25-Year summary of US malpractice claims for diagnostic errors 1986-2010: An analysis from the National Practitioner Data Bank. *BMJ Quality and Safety in Health Care*, 22, 672–680.

Sims, P. (2011). Little bets. New York, NY: Free Press.

Smith, J. M. (2013). Analyzing and Managing Data: The clinical nurse leader's role. In J. L. Harris, L. Roussel, & P. L. Thomas (Eds.), *Initiating and sustaining the clinical nurse leader role: A practical guide* (pp. 245-266). Burlington, MA: Jones and Bartlett Learning.

Soper, D. (2013). p-value calculator for correlation coefficients. Retrieved from http://www.danielsoper.com/statcalc3/calc. aspx?id=44

Swinford, E., & Terberg, J. (2013). *Building PowerPoint templates: Step by step with the experts.* Indianapolis, IN: Que.

Tufte, E. R. (1983). *The visual display of quantitative information.* Cheshire, CT: Graphics Press.

Tufte, E. R. (1990). *Envisioning information.* Cheshire, CT: Graphics Press.

Van Wye, G., Kerker, B. D., Matte, T., Chamany, S., Eisenhower, D., Frieden, T. R., & Thorpe, L. (2008). Obesity and diabetes in New York City, 2002 and 2004. *Preventing Chronic Disease: Public Health Research, Practice, and Policy*, 2, 1–15; appended tables, 1–5.

Wainer, H. (1997). *Visual revelations.* Mahwah, NJ: Erlbaum.

Weissman, J. (2003). *Presenting to win: The art of telling your story.* Upper Saddle River, NJ: Prentice Hall, 2003.

Wong, D. M. (2010). *The Wall Street Journal guide to information graphics.* New York, NY: WW Norton.

Yau, N. (2011) *Visualize this: The flowingdata guide to design, visualization, and statistics.* Indianapolis, IN: Wiley.

Yerkes, R. M., & Dodson, J. D. (1908). The relation of strength of stimulus to rapidity of habit-formation. *Journal of Comparative Neurology and Psychology*, 18, 459–482.

Zelazny, G. (2001). *Say it with charts* (4th ed.). New York, NY: McGraw-Hill.

Excel Chart Types and Variations

Column Charts

1. Clustered Column
2. Stacked Column
3. 100% Stacked Column
4. 3-D Clustered Column
5. Stacked Column in 3-D
6. 100% Stacked Column in 3-D
7. 3-D Column
8. Clustered Cylinder
9. Stacked Cylinder
10. 100% Stacked Cylinder
11. 3-D Cylinder
12. Clustered Cone
13. Stacked Cone
14. 100% Stacked Cone
15. 3-D Cone
16. Clustered Pyramid
17. Stacked Pyramid
18. 100% Stacked Pyramid
19. 3-D Pyramid

Bar Charts

1. Clustered Bar
2. Stacked Bar
3. 100% Stacked Bar
4. Clustered Bar in 3-D
5. Stacked Bar in 3-D
6. 100% Stacked Bar in 3-D
7. Clustered Horizontal Cylinder
8. Stacked Horizontal Cylinder
9. 100% Stacked Horizontal Cylinder
10. Clustered Horizontal Cone
11. Stacked Horizontal Cone
12. 100% Stacked Horizontal Cone
13. Clustered Horizontal Pyramid
14. Stacked Horizontal Pyramid
15. 100% Stacked Horizontal Pyramid

Line Charts

1. Line
2. Stacked Line
3. 100% Stacked Line
4. Line with Markers
5. Stacked Line with Markers
6. 100% Stacked Line with Markers
7. 3-D Line

Pie Charts

1. Pie
2. Pie in 3-D
3. Pie of Pie
4. Exploded Pie
5. Exploded Pie in 3-D
6. Bar of Pie

Scatter Charts

1. Scatter with only Markers
2. Scatter with Smooth Lines and Markers
3. Scatter with Smooth Lines
4. Scatter with Straight Lines and Markers
5. Scatter with Straight lines

Area Charts

1. Area
2. Stacked Area
3. 100% Stacked Area
4. 3-D Area
5. Stacked Area in 3-D
6. 100% Stacked Area in 3-D

Stock Charts

1. High-Low-Close
2. Open-High-Low-Close
3. Volume-High-Low-Close
4. Volume-Open-High-Low-Close

Surface Charts

1. 3-D Surface
2. Wireframe 3-D Surface
3. Contour
4. Wireframe Contour

Doughnut Charts

1. Doughnut
2. Exploded Doughnut

Bubble Charts

1. Bubble
2. Bubble with a 3-D Effect

Radar Charts

1. Radar
2. Radar with Markers
3. Filled Radar

Animating Charts in Powerpoint

There are three things to keep in mind in animating a chart. First and foremost, animation should not be used haphazardly but rather for a specific purpose. For example, use animation to allow for a sequential explanation of a complex chart or for dramatic effect (when the story calls for it). Second, select animation effects that are simple (like wipe, dissolve, or fade) and not dramatic. You don't want columns bouncing or flying into your chart! Third, if you opt to animate in a very detailed way (e.g., by element in category), realize that animating the entire chart will take a long time—in most instances, a *painfully* longer time than you would probably want to devote to one slide.

There are two ways to animate charts: The Chart Animation function built into PowerPoint and what I call the clunky way. I use the clunky way in most of my presentations.

PowerPoint Chart Animation Function

The PowerPoint Chart Animation feature allows you to introduce the chart grid and chart elements one at a time. Here's how it works.

A. Open a blank slide in PowerPoint and insert a chart—

the initial highlighted one, a clustered column chart, will be fine. Expand the slide view so it occupies the entire screen.

B. Click on the chart then the Animations tab.

C. Click on an animation effect—Wipe, the seventh from the left. When you select Wipe, you will see the entire chart wipe up from the bottom. The default in PowerPoint is to animate the chart as one object.

D. To animate chart elements individually, click on Animation Pane in the Animation ribbon. This will display a window on the right that will contain an entry for the chart.

E. To animate individual elements in the chart, click on the drop down box on the right side of the chart entry in the Animation Pane and select Effect Options | Chart Animation tab. A dropdown box next to Group Chart reveals five choices for animating the chart:

1. As One Object. All series for all categories appear at once.

2. By Series. All Series 1 as a group, followed by all Series 2, followed by all Series 3.

3. By Category. All Category 1 at once, followed by all Category 2, followed by all Category 3.

4. By Element in Series. Series 1 in Category 1, followed by Series 1 in Category 2, followed by Series 1 in Category 3. Repeated for Series 2 and Series 3.

5. By Element in Category. Series 1 in Category 1, followed by Series 2 in Category 1, followed by Series 3 in Category 1. Repeated for Categories 2, 3, and 4.
   If you select Options 2 through 5 above, there will

be an opportunity to determine whether you want the chart grid itself to be animated as the first step in the chart animation process. If you don't want the grid animated, uncheck the box for "Start animation by drawing the chart background."

The Clunky Way

An alternative way to animate charts (and other things) is to use slide transitions. Some reading this book, who only have an occasional need to animate a chart, may find it easier to use and to remember. Slide transition is the way that one slide in your slide show moves to the next slide. Even the most inexperienced PowerPoint user probably knows or can easily learn how to use PowerPoint slide transitions.

We'll look at a simple example but the same method can be used to animate more complex charts. Let's suppose that you wanted to animate the chart in Fig. B.1 so that the grid appeared first, followed by the columns for the first series (2010), and then columns for the second series (2011).

TIP

If you are unfamiliar with slide transitions, just Google "PowerPoint 2010 slide transitions," and several websites will appear that demonstrate the slide transition function.

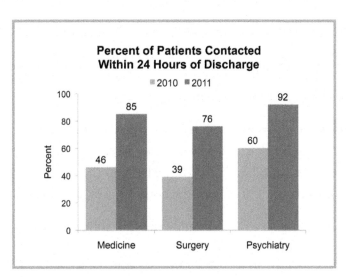

Fig. B.1. Column Chart to Be Animated

Here's how to animate this slide using slide transitions.

1. Create the slide you wish to animate. We'll use Fig. B.1.

2. In Slide Sorter view, highlight the slide, hit Copy | Paste. Now you have two copies of this slide.

3. Double click on the *first* of the two slides so that it is in the window by itself.

4. Double left click on one of the columns for the 2011 series.

5. When the Format Data Series box appears, click on Fill | No fill. The column fill disappears. Click on Border Color | No line. The column outline disappears.

6. Click on one of the 2011 Data Labels (all will be highlighted) and hit the Delete Key. The data labels for 2011 will be deleted.

7. Now you have two slides: the first with only the 2010 columns and data labels and the second with the 2010 and 2011 columns and data labels.

8. Duplicate the modified slide (the one with only the 2010 data), and on the first copy of this duplicate set, do the same for the 2010 columns (i.e., eliminate the fill, the outline, and the data labels).

9. Now you have three slides. The first has the chart grid (title, axis titles, and axis labels), the second has the columns and data labels for 2010, and the third has the columns and data labels for both 2010 and 2011.

10. Select Transitions | None for the first slide and select Transitions | Fade for the second and third slides.

11. Play the three slides in Slide Show. Notice how the grid appears (first slide), and then it appears as if the 2010 series are added to this first slide. In reality, you are showing a second slide, but it's not apparent to your audience because everything on the chart from the first slide remains, and the only "new" element is the presence of the columns for 2010. The third slide in the sequence introduces the columns for 2011.

    If the transition speed is too fast, you can slow it down by changing Duration on the Transitions ribbon. As I said, it's clunky, but it works and it's easy to remember.

Once you practice with this, you can animate almost any chart the clunky way. The downside is that you will have more slides in your presentation and you will have to delete all the "build" slides to create a handout.

Although there are a total of 58 different slide transitions to choose from, not all are suitable for animating a chart. You can use any transition effect in which it's not obvious that a different slide has been introduced. This would include cut, fade, wipe, random bars, and dissolve.

Parenthetically, slide transitions can also be used very effectively to animate items other than charts. Figure B.2 presents a flowchart showing a hypothetical disposition of patients who present at your Emergency Department. You're giving this presentation to a hospital-wide audience (staff from the ER, Inpatient Services, Outpatient Services, etc.) because you think it would be helpful for all staff to understand the entire process from beginning to end.

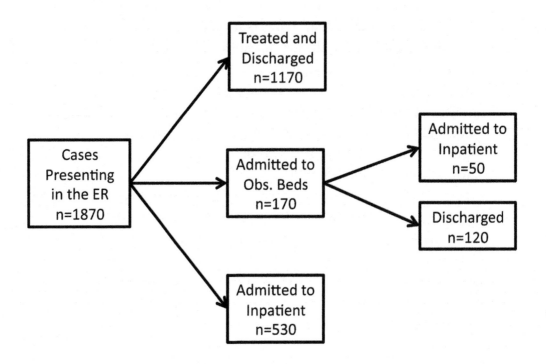

Fig. B.2. Flowchart of Cases Presenting in the ER

However, I'm sure you know what will happen as soon as you show this slide. Several in the audience will immediately scan the flowchart for their own particular area of interest and start thinking about that instead of listening to you as you work your way from ER presentation to the other routes. The way to prevent your audience from focusing just on the elements of interest to them is to animate this flowchart so that each item appears only when you are ready to discuss it.

While this flowchart can be animated using the built-in PowerPoint animation effects available on a single slide, it can also be animated the clunky way. Just create the *final, complete* slide (i.e., the one with all components). Duplicate this and delete the next-to-last box and arrow to be discussed. Duplicate this revised slide, and on the duplicate, delete the next item. Eventually you will have six slides, with the first in the series containing only the box for "Cases Presenting in the ER." The next slide will have that box plus the arrow and the box for "Treated and Discharged." The third slide will have these two boxes plus the arrow and the box for "Admitted to Obs. Beds." And so forth, until you get to the final, fully completed slide. The slide transition for all slides after the first one is wipe right. To your audience, it will appear that you are adding boxes to your original slide, rather than showing different slides.

Can the clunky way be used for items like pictures? It all depends on the picture. Try this:

1. Create a PowerPoint consisting of two blank slides.

2. On the Design tab ribbon, select Background Styles on the right and choose the fourth style, completely black. Both of your slides should now be completely black.

3. In your web browser, enter: http://www.nasa.gov/ multimedia/imagegallery/image_feature_2159.html

4. When the picture of the earth as seen from space appears, right click on it and select "Save picture as . . . ."

5. Use the picture name as it appears or rename it and save it to your computer.

6. On the *second* black slide of your PowerPoint, click Insert | Picture | locate the saved picture of the earth | Insert.

7. On the Transitions tab ribbon, select Random Bars as the slide transition for this second slide.

8. Play your Slide Show beginning with Slide 1.

Creating a Dot Plot in Excel With Category Labels on the Vertical Axis

If you have a frequently recurring need for creating dot plots with category names on the vertical axis, it's probably best to obtain a software program or an Excel add-on that would create these. However, if you only have an occasional need for this type of chart, you can easily create one if you are willing to do some hand work. Here are the steps.

1. Create a bar chart of the data (Fig. C.1).

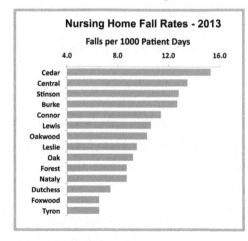

Fig. C.1. Bar Chart of Data

Bar charts should not have a truncated value axis but since we are converting this to a dot plot (which allows for a truncated axis), the value axis has been truncated.

2. Select a shape (e.g., a circle) and insert it in the chart. To create a perfect circle, hold the shift key down while drawing the circle. (Make sure that the chart area is highlighted when you enter the shape so that the shape is embedded in the chart.)

3. Duplicate the shape to create one for each of the bars.

4. Center one of these shapes over the ends of each of the bars (Fig. C.2). Removing the fill from the shape and enlarging the slide view with the zoom slider bar on the lower right of the screen will help to position these shapes precisely.

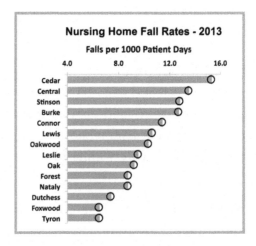

Fig. C.2. Bar Chart With Circle Shape Positioned at End of Each Bar

5. Remove the bars by double left clicking on a bar (this will highlight all bars) | Format Data Series | Fill | No Fill and Border Color | No Line. The bars and bar outlines will disappear.

6. If desired, fill the circles with a color. Select one circle by left clicking on it and then all others by pressing and

holding the ctrl key while left clicking on each circle in turn when a small plus sign appears next to the mouse pointer. All circles will now be highlighted. Right click on one of the highlighted shapes and, in the mini toolbar, choose Shape Fill | Black and Shape Outline | Black. You may highlight the facility of interest by right clicking on the desired circle | Shape Fill | Red and Shape Outline | Red. The resulting dot plot is presented in Fig. C.3.

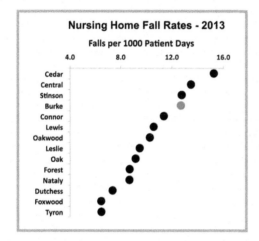

Fig. C.3. Final Dot Plot

Cylinder, Cone, and Pyramid Variations of Column and Bar Charts

In Excel there are a total of 34 variations of column and bar charts (19 column chart and 15 bar chart variations). Six of these were discussed in Chapter 4: clustered, stacked, and 100% stacked variations of both column and bar charts. What about the remaining 28 versions?

Seven versions of column and bar charts are designated in Excel as 3-D charts; these should be avoided. The remaining 21 column and bar chart variations are created by replacing rectangle shapes with cylinders, cones, or pyramids. Figure D.1 displays an Excel-labeled 3-D clustered column chart, along with three clustered column chart variations involving cylinders, cones, and pyramids.

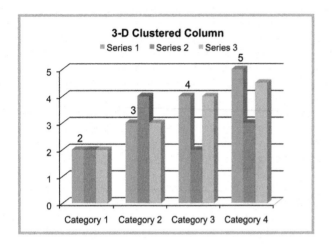

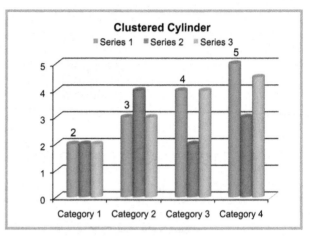

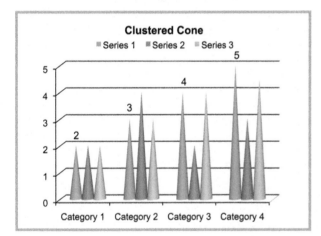

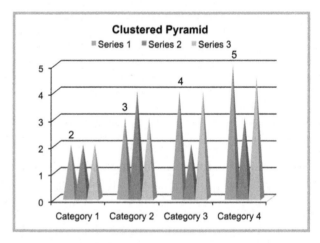

Figure D.1. 3-D Clustered Column and Clustered Cylinder, Cone, and Pyramid Charts

Note that only one chart in Fig. D.1, the first one, is designated in Excel as a 3-D chart. Yet, all charts in Fig. D.1 incorporate depth in shapes, the presence and depth of a side wall, a floor on which the shapes rest, and confusion of values with the grid in the background.

I'm not sure why there aren't 3-D designations in the names for all cylinder, cone, or pyramid variations. But of one thing I am sure: They are as much 3-D charts as the 3-D clustered column chart. For this reason, all 21 variations of column and bar charts that involve cylinders, cones, and pyramids should be avoided.

Basic Chart-Formatting Options

After you have selected the chart type and chart variation that best displays your information, there are a vast number of options for each of the individual elements in the chart (title, axes titles, axes labels, legend, data labels, colors employed, and the like). Jelen (2011) indicates that there are 780 quadrillion ways to configure a chart. This Appendix will focus on the basic options, the options you'll use most often.

There are three main ways to configure elements in your chart: adopting one of the preprogrammed arrays available in Excel, configuring chart elements individually, or a combination of both. These options are available through the use of the three Chart Tools tabs that appear on the ribbon whenever you click on a chart in PowerPoint or in an Excel spreadsheet. These three Chart Tools tabs are labeled Design, Layout, and Format. Many of the functions accessible through the use of these tabs are also accessible through the shortcuts described in Chapter 5.

Design Tab

Excel has tried to simplify the task of selecting options for individual elements in a chart by providing a number of preprogrammed formats. These preprogramed options for the chart type you have chosen can be found on the Design tab. Click on a chart and click on the Design tab. Two areas on this ribbon will be prominently displayed: Chart Layouts and Chart Styles.

Chart Layouts

Chart Layouts are preprogrammed combinations of chart elements (chart title, data labels, placement of the legend, use of a data table, etc.) in a variety of configurations. Some include a chart title, and some don't. Some have the legend on the side, some on the top, and some have no legend. Some have data labels, some don't, and some have a data table. You can click on the More arrow (a downward facing triangle with a line over it) for Chart Layouts to see what preprogrammed arrangements of components are available for that particular type of chart. The number of layouts varies depending on the type of chart you choose, from a high of 12 for line charts to a low of four for radar charts. If you see one that you like, select it and it will be applied to your chart. Although these are preprogrammed, once you select a layout, you can still modify an individual component of that layout if you choose.

Chart Styles

These are primarily color styles that you can apply to your chart. Eight different chart (color) styles are pictured across the top including grayscale, multicolor, and shades of different colors. Clicking on the More arrow on the right reveals that there are six rows of the eight columns, yielding a total of 48 different color styles for each chart type. Columns are numbered left to right: the first row, 1 to 8; the second row, 9 to 16; and so forth. Each column contains variations of the color palette in the first row, with each succeeding row in this column presenting a more complex style for this color palette. Figure E.1 presents some examples of these chart color styles for a clustered column chart.

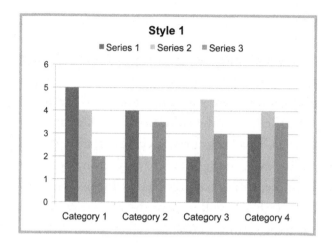

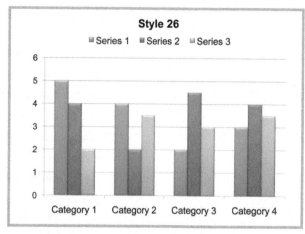

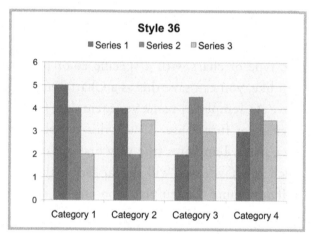

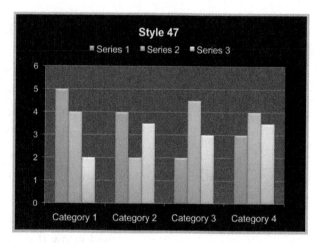

Fig. E.1. Examples of Various Chart Styles

Obviously, some of these chart styles are not ones that I would recommend since they involve considerable chart ink devoted to noninformation. In selecting a specific style, it would be wise to keep Wainer's caution in mind, "A graph that calls attention to itself pictorially is almost surely a failure" (1997, p. 11).

The Design tab also contains a number of other options.

Change Chart Type

The first option on the left of the Design ribbon, Change Chart Type, allows you to switch your chart from one type to another type. For example, if you want to see how your data looks as a line chart instead of a column chart, click on the column chart | Design tab | Change Chart Type | Line Chart | select the specific variation of line chart you want. Note, however, that not all chart types are compatible. It will not, for example, turn a column chart with two series of data into two pie charts. Rather, it will present the first series of data as a pie chart and ignore the second series.

Save As Template

If you design a specific type of chart with a specific color palette and specific options you like, you can save this as a Chart Template for future use. Select Save As Template | name your template | Save. The template will be saved for future use. To use this template in the future, select Insert Chart | Templates (the very first option) | a listing of templates which you have saved will appear | select the one you desire. It's helpful if you name the template you created with a descriptive name, rather than a generic "Template 1," so that you will know the format of the template from the name.

Switch Row/Column and Select Data

These options allow you to switch rows and columns or to add or delete data elements. More can be found on these options in books on Excel.

Edit Data

This option displays the spreadsheet of your data and allows you to add or delete columns or rows; change column or row headings; and add, change, or remove data.

Layout Tab

The Layout tab of Chart Tools is the place where you will find the most comprehensive array of options for changing the format of individual elements in a chart. Table E.1 presents an overview of the chart element format options and the types of charts to which they apply. As indicated, not all options are available for all charts. When you select a chart, only the options available for that type of chart and specific variation will be active; the others will be grayed out.

Table E.1. Format Options Available for Each Type of Chart

	Column	Line	Pie	Bar	Area	Scatter	Stock	Surface	Doughnut	Bubble	Radar
Chart Title	■	■	■	■	■	■	■	■	■	■	■
Axis Titles	■	■		■	■	■	■	■		■	
Legend	■	■	■	■	■	■	■	■	■	■	■
Data Labels	■	■	■	■	■	■	■		■	■	■
Data Table	■	■		■	■		■				
Axes	■	■		■	■	■	■	■		■	■
Gridlines	■	■		■	■	■	■	■		■	■
Plot Area	■	■		■	■	■	■			■	■
Chart Wall								■			
Chart Floor	Only with 3D Variations							■			
3-D Rotation								■			
Trendline	■	■		■		■	■			■	
Lines		■			■		■				
Up/Down Bars		■					■				
Error Bars	■	■		■	■	■	■			■	

Here's a brief description of each of the formatting options available for a multiple series line chart since this chart type has the most options available. Keep in mind that the options listed below for horizontal and vertical axes are determined by the type of chart created, in this case a line chart.

Chart Title Options

None, Centered Overlay Title (overlay centered Title on chart without resizing chart), or Above Chart (resize chart and display Title above chart plot area). The last title option—Above Chart—is the most commonly chosen one. You can choose the Centered Overlay Title, which places the title within the plot area, only if the display of data within the chart allows room for this.

Axis Title Options

Primary Horizontal Axis: None or Title Below Axis.
Primary Vertical Axis: None, Rotated Title, Vertical Title, Horizontal Title. Rotated Title is the most preferred option. Vertical Title, with the letters one above the other, is often difficult to read and a Horizontal Title often takes up too much space.

Legend Options

None, Show (Right, Top, Left, or Bottom), Overlay Legend (Right, Left). The overlay legend options place the legend within the plot area; you can subsequently relocate it anywhere within the plot area by dragging it with the mouse. Obviously, it can only be used if the pattern of data leaves room for it in the plot area. Placing the legend on the left or the right of the chart takes space away from the chart, and for this reason, it is preferable to place the legend on the top or bottom of the chart.

Data Label Options

None or placement Center, Left, Right, Above, Below the data point. The best position depends on the pattern of your data. Remember that these are the options for a line chart. Descriptions of options for other types of charts may vary. You can move an individual label with the mouse by left clicking on it to highlight all labels in this series, left clicking on it again to select just that label, and dragging it to the desired position with the mouse.

Data Table Options

None, Show Data Table, Show Data Table with Legend Keys. As indicated previously, data labels are preferred over a data table.

Axes Options

Primary Horizontal Axis. None, Show Left to Right Axis, Show Axis without Labeling, Show Right to Left Axis. The most commonly used, and the default, is Show Left to Right Axis.

Primary Vertical Axis. None, Show Default Axis, Show Axis in Thousands, Show Axis in Millions, Show Axis in Billions, Show Axis with Log Scale. The quantitative options are generally used with financial numbers like budgets, but they could be used with transactional data (e.g., 657,164 outpatient visits). Log Scale transformations are used when data have a very wide range and when one is interested in comparing rates of change rather than absolute change. You can find more information on these in a number of sources (Few, 2012; Harris, 1999; Jelen, 2011; Robbins, 2005).

Gridline Options

The options are the same for Primary Horizontal Gridlines and Primary Vertical Gridlines: None, Major Gridlines, Minor Gridlines, Major and Minor Gridlines.

Plot Area Options

None, Show Plot Area. The plot area is the rectangle formed by the horizontal and vertical axes. A plot area fill is not recommended; it conveys no information and sometimes makes the chart more difficult to read.

Chart Wall, Chart Floor, and 3-D Rotation Options

These options are available only with a Surface Chart or with a 3-D variation of another chart type. These options are a lot of fun. You can add colors to the walls and to the floor beneath the columns. You can rotate the chart like a top, or change the perspective, or view it from above for even from below the floor.

There's only one thing you can't do with these 3-D options, and that is to enable a 3-D chart to communicate information quickly and easily to most observers. So, if you want to play around with them to see what they do, that's fine, but remember it's just for fun.

Trendline Options

None, Linear Trendline, Exponential Trendline, Linear Forecast Trendline, Two Period Moving Average, in addition to other trend lines. If the chart involves more than one series of data, you can specify which series you want to use for the trend line, and you can have separate trend lines for each series if desired. Once you have selected the trend line, you can also include the equation for that trend line and the R-squared value in the chart.

Lines Options

None, Drop Lines, High-Low Lines. Drop lines insert a line from the data point to the x-axis; High-Low lines draw a line between the highest and lowest values for each of the x-axis categories. I have never had occasion to use these.

Up/Down Bars Options

None, Up/Down Bars. Draws a bar between the highest and lowest values for each x-axis category with the color of the bar changing dependent on which series is higher. I have never had occasion to use these.

Many of the Layout Tab options listed above also have More Options which allows you to change other aspects such as color, fill, and the like. The Layout tab also contains options for inserting pictures, shapes, or text boxes into your chart. If you insert these items by selecting them in the Layout tab, they will automatically be embedded in the chart.

Format Tab

The Format Tab of Chart Tools includes options to change Shape Styles, to use WordArt Styles, and to Arrange various elements in the chart. It also includes an area to specify the height and width dimensions of a chart. The latter is very useful if you want to assure that multiple charts are exactly the same size, as in Fig. E.1.

Inserting Charts Created In Excel Into Powerpoint

There are fifteen different ways to insert (i.e. paste) a chart created in Excel into a PowerPoint presentation. Presented below are three of these paste options: Options 1 and 2 will not update the PowerPoint chart with subsequent changes made in the original spreadsheet; Option 3 will update the chart. All begin by first copying the chart on the Excel spreadsheet.

1. *Keep Source Formatting and Embed Workbook.* If you select this option in the PowerPoint Paste drop down box, the chart and the Excel workbook will both be embedded into PowerPoint. The original Excel file can be changed or deleted and it will have no effect on the PowerPoint chart or its data which must now be modified within PowerPoint using the Chart Tools options.

2. *Paste as Picture.* If you select this option in the PowerPoint Paste drop down box, the chart will be pasted as a static picture exactly as it appears in the original spreadsheet. The data and the chart format cannot be modified using the PowerPoint Chart Tools.

3. *Paste as Link.* If you select Paste Special in the PowerPoint Paste drop down box, you will be given the option to paste a Link to the original spreadsheet as a Microsoft Excel Chart Object. In this instance, the chart in PowerPoint becomes a virtual shortcut to access the original Excel workbook, which must be a saved file. When you open the PowerPoint, you will be asked if you want to update the link. If you answer yes, any changes to the chart on the original Excel chart spreadsheet (both data and format) will be incorporated in the chart in PowerPoint. If you answer no, the chart will not be updated. If the Excel file is deleted or if it is not in the same file folder as the PowerPoint, there will be no link and hence no access to the data or Chart Tools.

The Excel Color Palette

The color of elements in a chart (e.g., columns, lines) can be changed by selecting one of the Chart Styles in the Chart Tools | Design tab. They can also be changed individually. For example, to change the color of columns in a column chart | double left click on one of the columns | Format Data Series | Fill | Solid Fill | Color. The Color dropdown box will reveal an array of Theme Colors and Standard Colors. An option for More Colors will produce a pop up box with two tabs: Standard and Custom. (The color palette can also be accessed by right clicking on the element you which to change and selecting the fill icon on the mini toolbar.)

Standard Color Tab

This tab contains a hexagon of 127 different color variations and a two-row display of 16 shades of light gray through black. Selecting any one of these color samples will display that color in comparison with the current color in a box on the lower right of the tab. Selecting this color will apply it to the selected element of your chart. You can change the color of lines and shapes by following the same steps.

Custom Color Tab

This tab presents a color box display with a rainbow array of colors.

You can move the cursor to define precisely the color you want. Moving the cursor left to right will change the color (i.e., the hue) while moving the cursor top to bottom will change the purity of the color (i.e., the saturation). Moving the vertical slide to the right of the rainbow box up or down will change the amount of gray added to the mix (i.e., the brightness) from white to black.

You can also enter specific numeric color values in the areas indicated beneath the rainbow display. There are a number of different coordinate systems used to define a specific color. Below the rainbow box, the RGB (red, green, blue) coordinates for this color are displayed. If you move the cursor in the color box, you will see changes to these RGB values. If you click on the dropdown box for Color Model, you can switch to another coordinate system, the hue saturation lightness system, with the HSL coordinates representing the same color.

If you want to duplicate a color used in another chart or in any other material on your computer screen, there is a helpful routine named Pixie that will enable you to determine the RGB values for this color. It is available free online from Nattyware (www.nattyware.com). Once activated, it produces a small box on your computer screen (Fig. F.1).

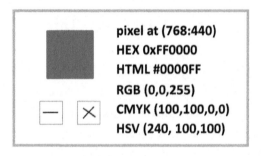

Fig. F.1. The Pixie Icon

When you move the mouse anywhere on the screen, this box tells you the precise pixel location of the cursor, displays the color at that location, and lists the RGB values for that color along with other color system designations. If you want to fill an element in your chart with that particular color, simply enter the RGB values in the places indicated for color selection as described above.

Formatting a Chart With Zero in The Middle of the Y-Axis

In a line or column deviation chart, the default position of the x-axis baseline and labels is at the zero point on the y-axis, that is, somewhere in the middle of the y-axis. In Fig. 6.3, for example, where the y-axis range is from -10 to +15, the lines and columns obscure some of the x-axis labels.

One way to correct this problem is to move the x-axis labels to the bottom of the chart while leaving the x-axis baseline at the zero point as a reference line. *This will work for both line and column deviation charts.*

Double left click on the x-axis labels | Format Axis. Near the bottom of the Format Options box is an option for Axis labels with the phrase "Next to Axis" adjacent to it. Use the dropdown box to change this to "Low." This will move the x-axis labels to the bottom of the chart while the baseline remains at the zero point. To remove the tick marks from the x-axis baseline, while the Format Options box is still open, look for "Major tick mark type" and a dropdown box containing "Outside." Change this to "None," and the tick marks will be removed from the x-axis baseline. You can also use this Format Options box to change the thickness of the baseline (Line Style) and its color (Line Color). The chart will now have the x-axis labels on the bottom and the baseline will appear as a reference line at the zero point.

An alternative method is to double left click on the *other* axis (the y-axis, the one whose position you don't want to change). The Format Axis box will appear and near the bottom there will be a section labeled "Horizontal axis crosses:." Select "Axis value" and in the adjacent box, enter the lowest value of the y-axis, in the case above -10. The x-axis (labels, baseline, and tick marks) will be moved to the bottom of the chart.

If you want the zero value line to appear darker or in another color as a point of reference, you must add another data column to your data sheet with zero entered for every x-axis category. This will create a second series, a straight line with no markers, across all x-axis categories at the zero value point. You can color or thicken this reference line as you wish.

This alternative method will not work for column deviation charts. Since columns are always drawn from the baseline, if you move the x-axis baseline to the bottom of a column deviation chart, the columns will be drawn up from the baseline (-10 in this case) toward and sometimes through the zero point on the y-axis.

Figure G.1 shows deviation charts produced using the methods described above. The column deviation chart was created using the first method. The x-axis labels have been moved to the bottom of the chart but the baseline remains at the y-axis zero point and serves as a reference line, extending from the y-axis line to the end of the chart plot area. The line deviation chart was created using the alternative method. Note how the x-axis labels and baseline have been moved to the bottom of the chart; the zero point reference line was created using a second data series and extends only for the range of x-axis categories.

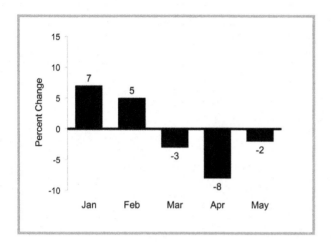 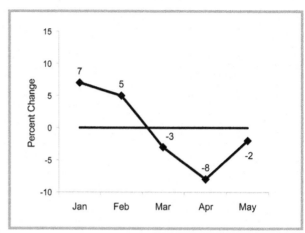

Fig. G.1. Line and Column Deviation Charts with X-Axis
Labels at the Bottom

APPENDIX

Additional Scatter Chart Topics

What Is the Least Squares Regression Line?

The least squares regression line is the straight line that fits your data best. It's called "least squares" for a very simple reason. If you were to draw a vertical line (i.e., parallel to the y-axis) from each of the points on your scatter chart to this line (the red lines in Fig. H.1), measure the length of each of these lines using the y-axis scale, square each of these lengths, and sum these squared values, this sum would be a specific number. In the case of Fig. H.1, this value is 22.04.

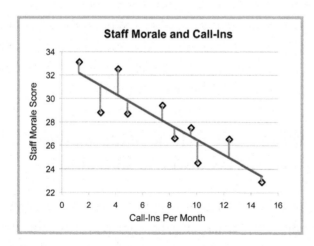

Fig. H.1. Deviations of Plotted Points From Least Squares Regression Line

TIP

Deviations from predicted values are referred to as residuals. Statisticians often plot the size and direction of these residuals at points along the x-axis to detect non-random patterns in these residuals. If a non-random pattern is detected, it suggests that the fitted line may not be the best fit for the data.

If you were to change the position of the line in any way (rotate it slightly clockwise or counter clockwise, place it slightly higher or slightly lower), and recalculate the sums of squares as described above, the sum would be larger than 22.04. That's why this line is referred to as the "least squares" regression line—any other placement of this line would yield a larger sum of squares.

The equation for the straight line in Fig. H.1 is:

$$y = -0.65x + 33.01$$

Excel computes this automatically, and you can insert it in your chart if you like. Click on the chart | Layout | Trendline | More Trendline Options | Display Equation on chart. It may seem like an awfully obtuse equation, but it's really very simple.

The first part of the equation for a straight line ($-0.65x$ in the example above) answers the question, "How much does the y value change for a given change in the x value?" If you look at Fig. H.1, you will note that as the value of x increases, the value of y decreases. In fact, the equation for the least squares line shows that y will decrease by 0.65 unit for every 1.00-unit increase in x. This is known as the slope of the line.

The second part of the equation for a straight line (33.01 in the example above) answers the question, "What is the value of y when x is zero?" In Fig. H.1, if you project the trend line to the point where the x value is zero, you will see that the y value is approximately 33 when the x value is zero. This is known as the intercept.

What's the Relationship Between the Slope and the Correlation?

The slope and the correlation may be viewed as analogous to military planes flying in formation. The slope represents the direction in which the planes are flying (positive correlation = northeasterly direction, negative correlation = southeasterly direction). The correlation represents the closeness of the planes to the flight path (high correlation = close formation, low correlation = loose formation).

Can you Fit Curves (Nonlinear Trend Lines) in Excel?

Yes, Excel gives a number of options for curve fitting. Click on chart | Layout | Trendline | More Trendline Options. It doesn't automatically select the curve of best fit for your data. You have to examine the pattern of data, guess at a best fit line, and see how that fits. For example, the curve in the Yerkes-Dodson data (Fig. 8.2) was a polynomial curve with an order of 2. As noted in the TIP on the previous page, statisticians use plots of residuals to determine whether the fitted line is a good fit for the data.

R-Squared Value

Excel can display an R^2 value for the data in the scatter chart. Click on the chart | Layout | Trendline | More Trendline Options | Display R-squared value on chart. Each of two variables has three components: the variability they share in common, the variability due to other causes, and error.

The R^2 value is the squared correlation coefficient, and it indicates the amount of variability that the two variables share in common. If the correlation is 0.90, the two variables share 81% of their variability in common (0.90 × 0.90 = 0.81). However, when the correlation is 0.30, the proportion of their variability that they share in common is only 9% (0.30 × 0.30 = 0.09).

Index

CPSIA information can be obtained
at www.ICGtesting.com
Printed in the USA
BVOW07s1103140517
483864BV00001B/2/P